KU-998-736

Separation Revisited
Adolescents in foster family care

Celia Downes

NOTTINGHAM
UNIVERSITY LIBRARY

*a*SHGATE

© Celia Downes 1992

All rights reserved. No part of this publication may be reproduced, stored in a retrieval system, or transmitted in any form or by any means, electronic, mechanical, photocopying, recording, or otherwise without the prior permission of the publisher.

Published by
Ashgate
Ashgate Publishing Limited
Gower House
Croft Road   I000650612 T
Aldershot
Hants GU11 3HR
England

Ashgate Publishing Company
Old Post Road
Brookfield
Vermont 05036
USA

A CIP catalogue record for this book is available from the British Library and the US Library of Congress.

ISBN 1 85742 042 X

Laserset by Computype Manuscript Services,
Standard House, Lawrence Street, York YO1 4BU

Printed and bound in Great Britain by
Billing and Sons Limited, Worcester.

SEPARATION REVISITED

Contents

List of tables

Acknowledgements

I would like to express my warmest thanks to the adolescents, foster parents, project social workers and senior management of the social services department where the study took place; I have chosen not to identify them in order to give additional anonymity to the adolescents and their foster parents. The inevitable loss is that I am unable to name many people who gave generously of their time and from whom I learned a great deal. The social services department supported a long term research project when they were under heavy work pressures and financial constraints, this included meeting the expenses incurred in the course of the research. A travel grant from the Hilden Charitable Foundation enabled me to arrange a study tour in North America which provided a stimulus from confronting similar issues in a different culture.

A major debt is to Dr John Bowlby who acted as a consultant to the study and constructively criticised some of the chapters. He had agreed to write a forward to the book but died before it was completed. The book is a tribute to him and particularly to his concern for young people in care and his appreciation of and respect for the complex task facing social workers, foster parents and other caregivers.

Thanks are also due to Professor Dorothy Whitaker for her invaluable advice, criticism and encouragement throughout the research; to Dr Dorothy Heard, Dr Brian Lake, Mrs Lyn Clarkson and Beth Williams for their constructive criticism of my drafts; to my colleagues who took on extra work in order to allow me time to finish the book and particularly to Professor Ian Sinclair for his unfailing support, encouragement and valuable, if astringent criticism.

For permission to quote from published material, thanks are due to the following publishers and authors: The Hogarth Press and the Institute of Psycho-Analysis, in respect of *Attachment and Loss:* Vol. 2, *Separation: Anxiety and Anger*, by J. Bowlby; The Society for Research in Child Development, Inc. at the University of Chicago Press, in respect of 'Security in Infancy, Childhood and Adulthood: a Move to the Level of Representation' by M. Main, N. Kaplan and J. Cassidy, in *Growing Points of Attachment Theory and Research,* edited by I. Bretherton and E. Waters; the University of Nebraska Press, in respect of 'Open Communication and Internal Working Models: Their Role in the Development of Attachment Relationships' by I. Bretherton, in *Socioemotional Development. (Nebraska Symposium on Motivation, 1988)* edited by R. Thompson; the *Journal of Family Therapy* for permission to quote from 'Family Systems and the Attachment Dynamic' by D.H.Heard.

Part 1
PERSPECTIVES ON FOSTER CARE FOR ADOLESCENTS

1 Introduction

This is a book about the relationships that develop between adolescents who are looked after by the local authority and their foster parents. It explores what it is like for them living under the same roof and sharing their lives together, having met for the first time when the adolescents are between 14 and 17 years old. By starting from foster parents' and adolescents' own accounts of what actually happened during time limited placements, the aim is to provide a way of understanding how they interact and what determines the course of the placement.

The book also offers ways of understanding and applying attachment theory to work with adolescents, both those in specialist fostering projects and those experiencing other forms of care. This is a new departure. In the field of family placement, attachment theory has indeed been used to explain the impact of insecure attachment, separation and loss on young children. It has provided a guide to decision making and action when helping children move into new families, (Fahlberg, 1981a, 1981b, 1982; Jewitt, 1984) and in managing behavioural problems once they are placed. (Fahlberg, 1988). It has also been used to understand the developing relationships between 5 to 9 year old boys and their substitute parents during the first year of permanent placements (Rushton, Treseder and Quinton, 1988). Nevertheless it has been criticized as offering an inappropriate or misleading perspective when applied to adolescent fostering (Hipgrave, 1989).

In this book, in contrast, attachment theory is applied to the fostering of adolescents. It provides a perspective for making sense of the powerful dynamics which frequently determine the outcome of a placement and suggests ways in which foster families, social workers and other practitioners may help or hinder adolescents' efforts to make constructive use of their placements.

The book is written for social worker practitioners and practitioners of other disciplines working with adolescents who are in care as the subject of a court order or are being provided with accommodation by the local authority, it is also for specialist foster parents and for practitioners working with foster families or with adolescents' own families. Much of it has wider application, for instance, to work with adolescents in small residential units and in their birth or reconstituted families.

This is not a comprehensive guide to all aspects of adolescent fostering, these are provided elsewhere, for example by Thoburn, (1988), and Aldgate, Maluccio and Reeves, (1989). It is not the intention to work through all the main issues which preoccupy adolescents; for example, negotiations concerning their developing sexual relationships and friendships are not explored. Nor does this book examine the crucial issues of race and gender and the adolescents' developing racial, cultural and religious identity. It is critical that these issues are considered in conjunction with the framework presented here, but this is too important a matter for a book of the size and form envisaged.

The aim is to offer a framework for understanding the relationships which develop between adolescents and foster parents and in particular the negotiations between them as adolescents move to and fro across the foster family boundary and sometimes move between their foster family and birth family. These negotiations raise issues of separation and attachment which are of importance to many adolescents but particularly for those who have had the past experiences of separation characteristic of foster children. Particular issues and events, such as finding work, and looking for a home base against the time when the placement ends are selected to explore and illustrate these negotiations; from these certain principles emerge, which, it is argued, are of considerable importance for all who work in this field. These principles have implications for understanding and assessing adolescents and foster parents, and for identifying ways in which adolescents, their birth families, foster parents, social workers and other professionals within statutory or voluntary agencies are most likely to work together effectively.

Developments in the practice of foster care

Developments in adolescent fostering have taken place during a period when there has been a general move on the part of local authorities from institutional to family care for children and young people. There has been an emphasis on the need to provide each child with a permanent home, either through enabling their birth family to provide this or through providing them with a new family. In practice this has led to a more extensive use of adoption and the severance of ties with the family of origin. Alongside this it has also been recognized that placement in residential care or in specialist, time limited foster care is an alternative which is more likely to meet the needs of some young people. Foster care has been considered appropriate for those coming into care in adolescence, who have strong links with their birth family, as well as for those who have spent a lifetime in care, and have experienced a series of disrupted placements (Berridge, 1985; Thoburn, 1988). However, these trends need to be set in the wider context; in their survey of placement patterns, Rowe, Hundleby and Garnett (1989) found that the proportion of children being fostered still drops rapidly with age and that most adolescents still go into residential care.

This general development of foster care is likely to be influenced by the new Children Act, although it is difficult to be clear at this stage precisely what form this influence will take. The philosophy and principles within the Children Act 1989 and the accompanying *Guidance and Regulations, Volume 3, Family Placements* (Department of Health, 1991) have developed out of the experience of the past ten years and are leading to new expectations and emphases. In order to be clear what is in the child's best interests, the wishes and feelings of children and their parents should be taken into account in planning and decision making. The emphasis on enabling children and their relatives to keep in touch with each other during separations and the concept of parents retaining responsibility for their children while they are being looked after by the local authority is likely to result in subtle changes in the relationships between foster parents, children and birth parents and in the ways in which they tend to view one another.

Foster parents, on their part, are given added powers to apply direct to the courts for a Residence Order in respect of a child who has been with them for more than three years in the last five and this will provide a less radical alternative to adoption in cases where a foster parent has become a child's primary attachment figure. These developments will require foster parents and birth parents to work together on behalf of separated children, and will require social workers to develop sophisticated skills to enable them to do so.

The developing autonomy of young people is recognized more clearly than has been the case in previous legislation and once a young person reaches the age of 16 years, the local authority may make a direct agreement with him or her to provide accommodation, despite parental objection. Aftercare is given increased prominence, in recognition of the lengthy process of transition from childhood to adulthood. Up to the age of 21 years, 'the support provided should be, broadly, the support that a good parent might be expected to give' (Department of Health, 1991, p. 91). The emphasis is on helping young people to develop the capacity for making satisfactory relationships, encouraging foster parents and other caregivers to maintain contact and interest in adolescents and young adults whom they have cared for, as well as encouraging young people to extend their friendship networks to include people outside the care system. Enabling young people to develop self esteem and to acquire practical and financial skills and knowledge is also recognized as important.

Fostering is recognized as a skilled task requiring training, it is suggested that it may sometimes be more appropriate for those who foster to be called foster carers or caregivers. This advice has not been followed in this book which argues that the particular skills that are most effective with adolescents in foster care are parental skills, adapted to their particular needs and developmental stage. However, a strong practical argument for the alternative titles is that being looked after by a foster carer or caregiver may engender less feelings of rivalry, disloyalty or failure on the part of adolescents and their birth parents.

In summary, although it is too early to judge the impact of the

6

new legislation, it is clear that it will require sophisticated understanding and skills on the part of foster parents and social workers if the Children Act is to work as it is intended to work, in the best interests of children and young people.

Recent developments in adolescent fostering

Against this general background there have been specific developments in foster care for adolescents. The numbers of adolescents in care has been rising over the last twenty years and specialist fostering projects for adolescents who are experiencing a range of difficulties have constituted a significant development in the thinking about social work practice since the mid 1970's, even though the number of adolescents placed through specialist projects is still relatively small. Many adolescents who are now being placed in families would previously have been deemed 'unfosterable' by social workers. They include those who have been the subject of physical, sexual or emotional abuse, and others who have also experienced major loss or a series of separations from their birth families or other significant caregivers, both within and outside the statutory care system. Some have experienced there being no place for them in reconstituted families. Family placement is also being used as an alternative to custody for those high up on the 'tariff', and as an alternative to secure accommodation for adolescents who repeatedly run from residential establishments. Many of these adolescents have developed patterns of relating to other people which make them very difficult to live with; their behaviour alienates people, is destructive to themselves or others and often seems to have the effect of preventing them from entering into or sustaining close relationships.

Berridge (1985) identified these adolescents as forming a considerable proportion of the population of the twenty children's homes that he studied. He makes the point that alongside certain groupings of younger children, they have a range of clearly identifiable needs requiring different forms of care. The mix of children and adolescents in most children's homes militates against their needs being met effectively in these establishments.

There have also been major changes in fostering practice,

particularly in the way foster parents, birth parents and statutory and voluntary social work agencies view their working partnership, and in the emphasis on open, explicit agreements about the purpose of a placement and planning about how it is hoped to achieve these. Many foster parents, particularly those recruited for specialist projects, rightly regard themselves as highly skilled specialists, and many more may well be so, even though they may find it difficult to put into words just what it is they do which seems to work so well.

Models of foster care

The changes and developments in the policy and practice of family placement have taken place in the context of disputes over how we should think about fostering practice. The models of foster care for adolescents which have developed alongside practice (Cooper 1978, Hazel 1981, Shaw and Hipgrave 1983, Hoghughi and Hipgrave 1985, Aldgate, Maluccio and Reeves 1989) are equivocal about the usefulness of the notion of treatment. Cooper provides a clear description of the task as:

> ...helping the adolescent learn about himself and to discover how his personality and behaviour affect and are affected by a small group organised as a family. The foster parents are not performing a substitute parenting role in relation to these near adults who are living with them. (Cooper, 1978, p. 102).

Cooper (1978), Hazel (1981), Shaw and Hipgrave (1983) all point to the major influence of task-centred casework. (Reid and Epstein, 1972) although this has often tended to be implicit rather than explicit in practice. From this model they acquire their emphasis on the voluntary agreement of all the participants about the problems and tasks to be worked at, the need for shared goals and the importance of the adolescent taking responsibility for their own behaviour and participating in decision making and goal setting. These are key concepts in work with adolescents generally, and in particular with those who have developed a 'script' in which they see themselves as helpless victims of past circumstances.

Also drawn from Reid and Epstein is the principle of setting the duration of work from the outset in relation to the time estimated as necessary to work on particular tasks. This is more controversial, and more recently has been challenged, at least for some groups of adolescents who could otherwise benefit from family placement (Stein and Carey, 1986, pp. 158-159; Thoburn, 1988, p. 96). Enlarging our understanding of the dynamic processes at work between adolescent and foster parent enables us to differentiate those placements where pre-set time limits are likely to be helpful or unhelpful.

The task-centred model has provided an effective lever for shifting traditional British child care practice, which previously tended to regard family care as suitable for younger children and placed adolescents in residential, often institutional care. The model is helpful in guiding practice in certain ways, for example, in suggesting how a placement might be organized in the beginning, and who should be involved in decisions. It is less useful in guiding practice when difficulties emerge in the course of placements, and it does not constitute a model for conceptualising what actually happens in the interactions between adolescent and foster parents.

From the reports of the experiences of adolescents, foster parents and social workers, it is clear that fostering adolescents with difficulties is a risky, emotionally demanding venture for those taking part. Social workers find they cannot predict the course or character of a placement. Some adolescents whose behaviour has previously proved very difficult for residential social workers to manage, settle down and are no trouble with their foster parents. With others, difficult behaviours comes to light for the first time during family placement. Adolescents no less than foster parents and social workers may find themselves emotionally drained by the demands made on them and frequently it is the dynamic processes in the relationship between them that eventually comes to be experienced as the greatest difficulty of all, overriding the more specific behavioural difficulties which were identified at the start of the placement.

The need to conceptualise the relationship between adolescents and their foster parents is a theme running through the literature on adolescent fostering and has been expressed particularly in the search for an appropriate concept of parenting of adolescents. The

9

concept of substitute parenting is generally thought to be inappropriate for this age group. This view is supported by practitioners' experience that the majority of adolescents approaching foster care are adamant that they do not want their birth parents replaced by foster parents. Attempts on the part of foster parents to demand that a fostered adolescent 'choose' between them and their birth parents almost invariably cause distress, and often the disruption of the placement. Yet in the course of some, though not all placements, strong feelings of attachment and psychological bonding do develop, to the obvious benefit of the adolescent. As a way of describing what actually happens, rather than as a statement of intent, substitute parenting does not always seem so wide of the mark, and constitutes one reason for the relevance of attachment theory to the practice of fostering.

In its development out of empirical studies of young children in interaction with their parents, frequently their mothers, and when separated from them, attachment theory has become associated in many people's minds with a form of care that necessarily ties mothers to the pram and the nappy changing. When this association of ideas is applied to adolescent fostering practice, the implications are thought to be that a foster parent, probably a foster mother, would be expected to become the adolescent's psychological parent, that they would operate on a model of care that excludes birth parents and other relatives (Holman 1975, 1980) and that they would be encouraged to parent in an inappropriate manner that would exacerpate regressive, dependent behaviour in adolescents who were needing to learn to cope with confidence in a harsh adult world.

A further objection to attachment theory has been that it offers a 'pathology' or psychologically determinist model of development which implies a bleak outlook for those who have suffered emotional damage, with little likelihood of change for the better. As an alternative to this depressing prospect, the argument runs, it is better to base ones practice on a theory that emphasises adolescents' inner strengths and resources and capacity to take responsibility for the direction of their lives.

As an alternative to substitute parenting, Shaw and Hipgrave advocate 'behavioural parenting' which:

conceptualises the parenting task in terms of handling and communication skill or in the modification of particular forms of conduct (Shaw and Hipgrave, 1983, p. 69).

Shaw and Hipgrave's emphasis here is on what foster parents do, rather than on how adolescents experience them. Many workers find this emphasis helpful when, at the beginning of a placement, they are seeking to enable foster parents, adolescents and their birth families to define the tasks to be worked on. It seems to have less to offer when placements run into difficulties. From observations of what foster parents actually do that appears to be successful, an alternative to substitute or behavioural parenting is clearly needed. Banks and Grizzell (DHSS, 1984), for example, suggest one that they call 'community parenting', this more aptly describes a process which they see as having more in common with residential therapeutic units than 'foster parenting'.

The task of this book

The changes in the practice of fostering combined with disputes about the theoretical basis of fostering makes it all the more important to think clearly about what fostering can achieve and how it might achieve it. In general this book offers a different understanding and application of attachment theory from those implied in the criticisms of it that have been put forward by Shaw and Hipgrave (1983) and Hipgrave (1989) It challenges the position outlined above by showing how adolescents' attachment to their foster parents in time limited placements has enabled them to make changes for the better, to take responsibility for themselves and to become more confident in finding a place for themselves in the adult world. It will be argued that attachment theory does not support a pathology model, is not psychologically determinist and underpins practice that encourages adolescents to take responsibility for themselves.

The concept of foster parenting developed here involves the foster family offering the adolescent an experience of a secure base for reappraising and renegotiating significant relationships, for gaining confidence in the wider world and for developing a greater capacity for mature interdependence. This concept, which has both behavioural and emotional dimensions will be introduced

11

in Chapter 3 and discussed in more detail in Chapter 8. In Chapter 9 ways in which the components of care which are combined in this form of parenting vary with the foster family's pattern of functioning, are discussed.

Drawing on attachment theory and family systems theory, it is proposed that the underlying purpose of adolescent fostering is to enable adolescents to change course in the way they relate to the people who are closest to them. Even small changes can make a significant difference to the manner in which the key psychosocial tasks associated with the transition from adolescence to adulthood are negotiated and the quality of mature self reliance that is achieved. How far change for the better comes about depends on what both adolescent and foster family are able to bring to the relationship between them.

My aim in contributing to theory is to revise the existing model of adolescent foster care rather than to criticize it. In keeping with current theory, the emphasis is on the importance of adolescents choosing to join a family because they want to risk this emotionally demanding route to adulthood. In order for this to work, placements need to rely on joint decision making; all concerned must be clear about their expectations and continue to share these openly with each other. Adolescents do not have to be victims of their own scripts and it is both desirable and possible for them to take responsibility for their behaviour and their future.

Nevertheless, the focus is on the dynamic processes at work, which always constitute an undercurrent in such placements and which frequently assume an overwhelming importance, especially if they previously have not been attended to. Foster parents and social workers ignore interaction based on distorted patterns of attachment at their peril. By suggesting ways of understanding these processes, the aim is to provide guidelines on what is likely to constitute helpful intervention on the part of foster parents, social workers and other practitioners if family placements are to function reparatively for adolescents in care.

The role of the social worker

By focussing on what happens between foster parent and adolescent, the social worker is apparently moved off centre stage. This could be misleading if it is taken to imply that foster parents take over all the 'direct work' and social workers assume the marginal role of 'case managers', while the adolescent's birth family are regarded as no more than a token presence at reviews, contract meetings and case conferences. This is not the intention. The adolescent is part of a caregiving network which it is useful to view systemically. In addition to having statutory responsibilities towards the adolescent, the social worker's role is to enable the caregiving network to function in the best interests of the adolescent. This will involve an understanding of dynamic interaction in the whole caregiving system of which the adolescent is part and in its various subsystems, for example, those created between adolescent and foster parent or foster family, and foster parents and birth parents. This will be the focus in chapter 10.

In keeping with the emphasis on the caregiving system, it will be argued that it is unrealistic and a false economy to think in terms of one social worker working with both the adolescent and the caregiving system; the minimum that is likely to be effective is one social worker responsible for the adolescent and one working with the caregiving network. Once the principles are understood, the best arrangements are likely to combine clarity about the roles and tasks of each member of the network at a given point in the placement with flexibility and experimentation over new ways of sharing out the work to be done. It is essential to recognise that adolescent fostering is labour intensive, and requires a highly skilled team

The research and the project in which it was based

The book is based on an intensive study of interaction between fostered adolecents and foster family members in 23 time limited placements arranged by an adolescent fostering project in one local authority. The placements were selected on a 'first come, first served' basis, subject to the willingness of all concerned to collaborate in the research. The placements started between February 1979 and October 1981. From June 1980, only placements of girls were included in order to even up the numbers of girls and boys in the study.

The numbers to be included in the study were not fixed at the beginning since it was difficult to predict how many adolescents and foster families would need to be studied to reflect the range and diversity of adolescents, foster family structures, interactive styles etc. in the project. A decision to stop including additional adolescents and foster families was made when data had been collected on 28 placements. At this point it became clear that the data coming in from the interviews was no longer yielding essentially new information and understandings. A further 5 were excluded once data analysis was underway, this was because the very rich potential of the data for analysis in each case indicated the value of intensive analysis on fewer cases. There were various grounds for exclusion which are described in detail in the full account of the research study (Downes, 1986).

This left 11 placements which were studied at three monthly intervals throughout the length of the placement. These were all placements that continued long enough for a minimum of two research interviews, in some cases the second interview took place retrospectively after the placement had ended. Another 12 placements were studied at the point the placement ended. One boy featured in two placements, one in the prospective and one in the retrospective sample. While the placement was continuing, all interviews were with the foster family and adolescent together. When the placement had ended the participants chose whether to be interviewed together or separately. Over 100 such interviews were recorded on audio cassettes. They were analysed using methods which moved step by step from the raw data to a set of inferences about what was happening. The research methodology is summarized in Downes (1988).

The adolescent fostering project was organized and run centrally by a specialist team of social workers in a social services department. Foster parents were recruited specially for the project, they were paid a fee for their services that they regarded as reasonable for the job. Members of the specialist social work team selected and trained foster parents and worked with them in on-going support groups which were a requirement for all foster parents within the project.

The specialist social work team established criteria for admission of adolescents to the project; generally they were assessed as being, for whatever reason, unsuitable or too difficult to place in foster families who were not part of the adolescent

14

fostering project. The team also prepared the adolescents for placement, through groupwork extending over several consecutive days.

Area team social workers who referred adolescents to the project continued to carry statutory responsiblity for them through the placement, while a member of the specialist team was designated as having responsibility for providing support and consultation to a particular foster family. Together these two social workers made up part of the team concerned with the placement, which would also include the foster parents and adolescent and where possible the adolescent's birth parents. Aims, objectives and plans were worked out together by this group of people at the start of a placement and usually agreed in the form of a written contract which was reviewed at planned intervals through the placement. Placements were intended to be time limited and usually planned to last from six months to two years.

The contents of the book

The book is divided in three parts, of which Part 1 introduces the issues to be considered, part two provides the main research material and Part 3 draws out the implications of this material for theory and practice.

In keeping with this plan, Chapter 2 provides an overview of one placement, drawing on excerpts from the interviews with Tom Skipper and the Armstrong family. This is followed in Chapter 3 by an outline of the key theoretical ideas which underpin the study, illustrated by a discussion of some of the issues and events of Tom's placement.

In Part 2 negotiations across the family boundary between adolescents and foster parents around four key events are examined. These are:

1. The transition to school or work.
2. Interaction between adolescents and their birth families and foster families.
3. Interaction on reunion, following episodes of going missing.
4. The ending of the placement.

Each involves adolescents and foster family members negotiating with each other as the adolescent moves to and fro between the foster family and the world he or she inhabits outside the foster family. Using particular examples of interaction as illustration, a picture builds up of adolescents' characteristic patterns of interaction and of what members of the foster family bring to these negotiations which either helps or hinders the purposes of reparative change.

Part 3 draws together the theoretical and practical ideas that have been developed in Part 2 to provide a framework for understanding, assessing and working with the interaction between adolescents and their foster parents and the wider caregiving network that surrounds them.

2 Tom Skipper and the Armstrong family

By the time of the second research interview, Tom had been living with the Armstrong family for four months. Halfway through the research interview the conversation took an unexpected turn:

Tom   You know when John told me that you were going to write a book about this, he said 'she will talk about you but she won't mention your name'...and I wanted to request that you use my name...I would like you to mention my sister as well.

Interviewer   But what would you like the world to hear?

Tom   About my life.

Interviewer   Well you haven't really told me about that yet.

Tom   Well, I was born.

Mrs Armstrong You were under a gooseberry bush, definitely.

Tom   No. I was under a compost heap. When I was born my mum was a bit ill and she didn't really care for me much or feed me much and so I was very ill. And I first started, I went into care when I was four. Karen was about two when she went into care and we stayed in this nursery about a year and I couldn't speak until I was about four. I can remember the first word I ever spoke was a CAR.

17

Mr Armstrong	I bet you didn't say it that way.
Tom	A car, that's the only word I could say you see, and then I got some foster parents, and I got there and started to live with them, and a couple of weeks later when the foster mum started to be a bit nasty with me and my dad used to be really nasty, she used to belt me.
Mr Armstrong	This was the foster mother?
Tom	She used to get depressed a lot. She used to belt me with a belt if I did anything wrong like, sort of messed about...she used to get depressed and my foster mum sort of got ill. She got a heart attack and then she got another heart attack... It was a strong heart attack and she had to go into hospital you see and then she was alright and then she got another heart attack when I was eight, eight yes, and then she woke up one morning and she felt hungry, so she had something to eat and then she went upstairs and my dad heard this bang and she went.
Interviewer	Were you in the house at the time?
Tom	No, I was playing about. My dad told me, well my grandma told me what happened, that she had died. I said 'oh'. I wasn't really bothered.
Mr Armstrong	Though you'd lived there for four years?
Tom	Yes.
Mr Armstrong	All the time, you'd actually lived there?
Tom	Yes, grandma told me she'd died, you see.
Mrs Armstrong	You said you cried because Karen was crying.
Tom	Yes, I thought 'Karen's crying', so I just cried. I started to cry. It was just put on.
Mr Armstrong	You remember that? You remember that you did put it on?
Tom	Hm.
Mr Armstrong	Whew...Do you want to come over nearer the fire and sit here?

Tom's foster father returned to the West Indies and his foster grandmother took on the care of Tom and Karen. They lived a peripatetic existence as grandmother moved around the country keeping an eye on all her elderly relatives.

Tom continued:

> I started to be really nasty...I used to throw things at her...I used to steal money from her...I bought a cowboy suit, I bought my sister a game and I bought lots of sweets and my sister hid the money under my pillow and my grandma found it, was I in trouble! So she took the cowboy suit off me and she gave me the cowboy suit for my Christmas present...So on Christmas Day I started to sulk and be miserable and my grandma started to ignore me, so I got really mad; I went 'swish' with the television set, on the floor.

Tom wreaked havoc and destruction until his foster grandmother, by this time in her seventies, had had enough and asked for him to be removed. He was 10 years 6 months old; over the next five years the escalating spiral of mutual infuriation, destruction and recrimination which had built up between Tom and his foster grandmother was transposed to and amplified with the staff of four Childrens Homes.

When Tom had started to tell his story, he was sitting half outside the family circle. Even when John Armstrong invited him to come closer to the fire, he continued to shiver.

Tom had arrived just before his 16th birthday to spend two years with the Armstrongs. He would be due to leave them when he left care at 18 years. He was small, a bit like a slightly plump 12 year old choir boy. He smoked heavily. Deciding to come had seemed a risky decision for him:

Tom	I thought it might be awful, so I were real scared when I first came here. I thought you would be like foster parents.
Mr Armstrong	Ah, yes, but that was before you came. And now he's much more scared!
Interviewer	You expected it would be like your other foster parents?

Tom	Yer, I was real scared...and I seem to get nightmares now about things what's happened in the past...Like my foster mum and about things which she has told me and what I hadn't said. It's all forgotten now. She used to talk about things...everything you know and I used to get nightmares about that...When that wind starts to howl I start to shake.
Mr Armstrong	Well I'm afraid that sometimes in the winter it blows so hard that you can actually feel the pressure of the wind against the wall and you think 'Crikey, is it going to stand up to it?' It will.
Mrs Armstrong	John built this house you know...It's a bit worrying at times!

The strength of the walls of the house against the hostile elements, presents a powerful image. For Tom, it seems that the impact of this placement is to resurrect fearful memories from his past; yet Tom recounts these memories in a manner which is so emotionally flat that it is not clear whether he is repeating a story he has been told about somebody else.

The Armstrongs are attentive as Tom tells them his story, but they tend to keep their focus on what is happening between them and Tom during the placement.

Mr Armstrong	He still finds he has lots of ups and downs.
Mrs Armstrong	All the time really.
Mr Armstrong	But he is a very nice person. This is not flannel, I'm not just saying that. He's a very nice person at heart. There are times when we could...
Mrs Armstrong	Shall we take him out and throttle him now!
Mr Armstrong	We have a tendency to being pretty rotten to him really when he is being rotten.
Mrs Armstrong	He is infuriating really when he is...
Interviewer	In what way? How does he infuriate you?
Mrs Armstrong	Well, ask Tom!
Mr Armstrong	He digs his heels in and he is not in a very good position to dig them in you know...Well, I mean, the last sort of example of you digging your heels in about what you wanted to do and not what you should have done.

20

Tom	And what was that?
Mr Armstrong	When you decided that you were not going to go to work and it was because of something we had said. We had upset you somehow or other.
Mrs Armstrong	...you came back to pick Tom up at 1.45 pm to take him to work, and Tom likes to be taken to work at one minute to 2 pm don't you? And then he disappeared and we couldn't find him.
Tom	...and I thought 'damn it', so I walked sulking out right across the road and then I went to the castle and I sat down for about an hour and then I started to walk home and...I walked by your house and then I sat down on the green grass down there, right? I were thinking...I saw your landrover come...and you said 'Don't knock that wall down'.
Interviewer	What did you think about?
Tom	I thought how to get my revenge back on 'em.

The desire to repay injuries by inflicting hurt is, of course, powerful and dangerous and takes some handling if it is not to be translated into action. Although Tom's feelings were noteably absent when he recounted what had happened to him in the past, he is currently furious with the Armstrong's. We begin to sense here the risk involved for Tom and the Armstrongs and the importance of understanding what it is about the Armstrong's care which enables Tom to manage, without disaster, this fury.

By the time Tom had been living with the Armstrongs for seven months, his life had taken several important turns which suggested that the risks for him and the Armstrongs were worth taking. At the beginning of the placement, Tom's first experience of work had been as a part time worker in a local factory owned by Mr Thackwray, an acquaintance of the Armstrongs. Tom had seemed bored and exhausted by the work until he was offered a full time job on the staff.

Mr Armstrong commented:

> He was transformed almost overnight... from being a very difficult young boy doing part time to a sort of working man, within a matter of days of doing full time...I happened to bump into

> Mr.Thackwray [he] said ' My goodness...what a
> change in the lad. My, there's no flies on that
> lad...! Whereas if I'd spoken to him before, I
> think he would have been sort of despairing a bit.

With hindsight it was clear that by holding down a full time job,
Tom had achieved something of prime importance to him. At the
beginning of the placement when he first started in work, part
time, and returned home each afternoon bored and exhausted, it
would not have been easy to anticipate just how important this full
time job was to be for him.

Tom had also been getting to know his mother. He had retained
no memory of her; he probably had not seen her since he came
into care at 4 years old. His social worker had a hand in discovering
where she lived and was planning to accompany Tom and Karen
on their first visit. However they were too impatient to wait for
their social worker, and set out on their own one weekend. They
knocked on the door, introduced themselves and spent the day
with their mother and Joe, her partner, talking about the family.
Tom described what happened:

> We decided to stay all night, and Karen went up
> to bed with my mum, you know. She slept in the
> same bed and I slept on the couch and Joe slept in
> the chair, and then the police came.

The police came because Tom and Karen had not told anyone
they were staying overnight and Karen's foster mother had reported
her missing. Tom seems to have expected that an unsanctioned
visit to his mother and an equally unsanctioned overnight stay
might have dire consequences. Commenting on this incident Mr
Armstrong said:

> I think Tom was a bit torn about coming back, to
> be quite honest, and that's understandably so. He
> thought that we were furious with him, and we
> weren't of course, and he came back bewildered...

It is not surprising that Tom was bewildered. As well as returning
to his foster home with expectations coloured by his previous

experience of care, he was needing to make sense of his new perceptions of his mother, and he was wondering whether there might be a home for him with her when he left care. The Armstrongs were unpeturbed by Tom's unplanned overnight stay and were therefore able to belie his expectations that they would be furious with him on his return.

By the time Tom had lived with the Armstrongs for a year he had acquired a motor bike; though he never entered for his driving test; a portable television, a cassette recorder, a tent which he had used once and money in the bank. He was sleeping better and was no longer scared at night. He never missed a day's work.

But although Tom was no trouble and the Armstrongs were pleased that he was far less moody, they were not entirely happy about the uneventfulness of this period of the placement:

Mr Armstrong	He doesn't do anywhere near enough actually.
Tom	That's what you think, not what I think, no, John.
Mr Armstrong	It's the bone of contention between us. We actually feel that you really must start to make more effort to develop your own social life... You see at the moment Tom's weekends are really frittered away, literally. I'm not saying you don't enjoy them.
Tom	...You're just sick because you want me to go away.
Mr Armstrong	We're not talking about going away. I think you should do things in the town and around...I just don't think you're getting as much out of life at your particular age, you know, in enjoyment. I'm not talking about anything useful but I think you should be doing things that you enjoy more.

But what Tom enjoys, it seems, is the safe haven of the foster home. He is content to move between this and the now almost equally safe haven of his job, but he is not yet ready to move further afield, and his foster parents recognize this:

> You don't need a lot to make you content, do you, really? I mean, as long as you've got something to eat and something to drink and you've got some tele...provided you've got some cigs.

This sense of progress in the early stages of the placement followed by a plateau where little seems to happen, and carers become more acutely aware of an adolescent's limited capacity to relate to them and to his peers, has long been recognized by practitioners. More recently it has been identified in research into post-adoption experience, (Macaskill, 1986). Tom's foster parents continued to be concerned about how they could help him reach a point where he could manage the move away from them by the time he was due to leave care at 18 years.

Has Tom become over dependent on the Armstrongs? Is he stuck in the safe haven of this foster home? Should he be ejected to force him towards 'independence', the traditional goal of such placements? Might it have been more in Tom's interests to place him in an Independent Living Unit at 16 years, where he could spend his last two years in care learning the practical skills of physical survival?

How the Armstrongs and Tom's social worker answer these questions is likely to have some bearing on the way the placement ends and its outcome. On the one hand the Armstrongs recognized Tom's remarkable progress; Mrs Armstrong told him:

> I tell you what, whoever sent you here,...they didn't give you a cat's chance in hell of succeeding in anything, I don't think, well they are amazed that you have done so well.

On the other hand they were doubtful about Tom's readiness to leave care at 18 years, but they were working within a statutory system of care in which this was unavoidable. As Tom's 18th birthday drew closer. Tom and his foster parents settled for a caravan for him, which could be parked as close or as far away from them as Tom chose. Tom moved out to the caravan on his 18th birthday. It was parked in the lee of the house, sheltered from the strong winds that had troubled him at night in the early months of the placement.

Within two weeks of moving out, and Tom's successor moving in to the foster home, the two boys were involved in a series of thefts in the locality. These appeared to have been commited while they were glue sniffing. With the backing of his foster parents and employer, Tom narrowly escaped a custodial sentence. Tom said he did not think his behaviour had anything to do with moving out from the foster home. The Armstrongs found him defiant about the offences. Mrs Armstrong descibed how they struggled with their anger at Tom's behaviour and attitude:

> We weren't very nice to him...we didn't speak to him a lot and we left him on his own in his caravan for that weekend. He came over on the Monday and he said he didn't feel well and John said 'Why, what's the matter with you?' He said 'I feel depressed.'

At the final research interview, a month after Tom moved out, he was managing to look after himself and his caravan. He called on the Armstrongs briefly most evenings, but had not invited them to the caravan. Tom was asked what was the worst thing about moving out.

> Oh the worst thing is I've got to walk to work everyday...'cos John is on holiday now...Well, I said to John, 'I'll walk, 'cos you want a rest...'

So Tom's placement ended on an ambiguous note. In many ways he was functioning better now than when the placement started, and his final comment displayed a recognition of his foster father's need for a holiday and his willingness to accommodate himself. This is in marked contrast to his intolerance at being ferried to work fourteen minutes early at the beginning of the placement. Yet on the other hand, his responsibility for himself and his actions seems to have taken a severe hammering at the point the placement ended, and with it his new found capacity to draw on his foster parents resources at moments of high anxiety. In turn, the Armstrong's ability to feedback reflectively to Tom the impact he has on them, rather than to become furious, seems to have been somewhat shaken at this point.

Our understanding of the significance of these factors and our predictions as to the long term outcome of the placement will depend on the theoretical perspective adopted. Before commenting further on Tom, the theoretical framework which underpins this account of a placement are discussed in Chapter 3. Further comments on Tom's placement with the Armstrong's will be presented in that context.

3 An outline of the key theoretical ideas

This chapter outlines some of the key theoretical ideas which are used in this book to offer a perspective on what happens between adolescents and their foster parents during placements. These ideas are drawn mainly from attachment theory and family systems theory. They will be illustrated with references to Tom Skipper's placement with the Armstrong family, described in Chapter 2.

Adolescence as a life stage

Adolescence is a time for renegotiating relationships; in particular there is a shift from parents being the most significant attachment figures to partners and friends taking on this role. In practice this does not always happen steadily, and all in one direction. Peer relationships are likely to be formed and broken, or a friendship that is experienced as very important at one point may lose it's significance as an adolescent's school, college, workplace or interests change. The process may continue well into adult life, involving many returns to base when parents again become the preferred attachment figure for a time. Whether or not the transition is smooth or turbulent, relatively sudden or gradual, it will involve exploring the world outside the family to a much greater degree than at previous stages of development. Friendships with adults outside the family, teachers, youth leaders or adult colleagues, for example, sometimes provide a staging post or alternative base for an adolescent engaged in these emotionally demanding activities.

The process may be conceptualised more broadly as a series of psychosocial tasks, concerned with establishing a place in the world of adult work, establishing peer friendships and sexual relationships, reappraising childhood experience as well as renegotiating relationships with parents. Each task contributes to a developing sense of self through reorientation to a range of key relationships. Operations are extended outwards from the family so that a separate base is eventually established while links are usually maintained with the family of origin.

The emphasis on adolescents facing outwards, away from their family of origin, has sometimes led practitioners in the field of family placement to doubt the wisdom of placing older adolescents in care in foster families. Might it not be setting adolescents an unnecessary additional, complex task to place them in another family just at the point that they are separating from their birth families? In order to address this issue, it is useful to consider some of the processes that usually operate for adolescents who remain in their birth families.

Adolescents who have so far experienced parents or parent figures as reliably available when needed, are able to move in widening circles outside the family as they negotiate these psychosocial tasks and experience the anxiety concomitant with new learning and change. They can be confident that as they move to and fro across their family boundary, their earlier attachment figures will continue to stand behind them and come to their aid if need be. In the event of parents being no longer available, they have the capacity to seek and use help from other people. The process in which they are engaged can be regarded as a realistic preparation for adult autonomy, when this is understood not as a condition of splendid isolation but of mature interdependence.

The idea of mature self reliance, not as total independence, but as stemming from confidence in a secure base for exploration has been developed by Bowlby:

> For not only young children, it is now clear, but human beings of all ages are found to be at their happiest and to be able to deploy their talents to best advantage when they are confident that, standing behind them, there are one or

27

more trusted persons who will come to their aid should difficulties arise. The person trusted provides a secure base from which his (or her) companion can operate. And the more trustworthy the base and the more it is taken for granted, unfortunately, the more likely is its importance to be overlooked and forgotten (Bowlby, 1973, p. 359).

The adolescents we are considering are not able to take a secure base for granted. Taking Tom Skipper as an example, his early experience is marked by an absence of reliably available attachment figures. While the Armstrong family has the potential for developing into such a base for Tom, it is clear that he has considerable difficulty in experiencing them as reliable at the start of the placement. Tom even appears to be in danger of sabotaging his developing relationship with the Armstrongs by his furious wish for revenge when his needs are not met to the minute. Although he gradually comes to an increased appreciation of their reliability, it continues to be doubtful how far he is able to sustain this conviction when he is operating outside the foster family, and outside the very close knit supportive network which surrounds him at work. It may take a longer period of time than the length of the placement itself for Tom not only to experience the Armstrongs as a secure base when he is with them but also to internalise this experience so that he can manage equally well for long periods when he is not with them.

In line with statutory provision at the time of the study, Tom was due to leave care at 18 years of age. The time limited nature of the placement emphasises that it is intended as a transition between a career in care and survival without statutory support and protection. An implication of Bowlby's concept of a secure base as providing for a need we all have throughout life, is that Tom is likely to need easy access to his foster parents for some time to come. The Armstrong's understood this, but the manner in which the placement ended appeared to make it difficult for both Tom and the Armstrongs to keep in touch with each other on easy terms. There remain uneasy questions about how Tom's new found but very tentative confidence in his foster parents might continue to be sustained and nurtured through the transition of the end of the placement, and eventually be transferred into his approach to other relationships.

Foster placement as a critical junction on a developmental pathway

Time limited fostering during middle or late adolescence is introduced at a life stage where much, perhaps critical, development has already occurred. One's point of view about the course and pattern of early development and its implications for later development and for adolescents' capacity for change, must therefore be important. The model of work on which many time limited placements are based, which was described in chapter 1, has rightly emphasised that adolescents should be encouraged to take responsibility for their behaviour and for what they wish to achieve. As a corollary to this it has sometimes been argued that to dwell on the influence of adolescents' experience of past events is psychologically determinist, and encourages the adolescents themselves and others concerned with them to regard them as helpless victims of an unchangeable script.

It will be argued that for adolescents, appreciating the impact and influence of past events and taking responsibility for behaviour are not incompatible. Accurate knowledge and being fully in touch with feelings about what happened in the course of earlier traumatic events will enable them to begin to free themselves from their current influence. These different viewpoints rest on two different models of personality development. Bowlby (1973) makes use of an analogy to contrast them:

> These two, alternative, theoretical models can be likened to two types of railway system. The traditional model resembles a single main line on which are set a series of stations. At any one of them, we may imagine, a train can be halted, either temporarily or permanently; and the longer it halts the more prone it becomes to return to the station whenever it meets with difficulty further down the line.
>
> The alternative model resembles a system that starts as a single main route which leaves a central metropolis in a certain direction but soon forks into a range of distinct routes. Although each of these routes diverges in some degree, initially most of them continue in a direction not very different from the original one. The further each

29

route goes from the metropolis, however, the more branches it throws off and the greater the degree of divergence of direction that can occur. Nevertheless, although many of these sub-branches do diverge further, and yet further, from the original direction, others may take a course convergent with the original; so that ultimately they may even come to run in a direction close to, or even parallel with, routes that have maintained the original direction from the start (Bowlby, 1973, p.365).

Both models imply a destination which Bowlby formulates as 'a person who approaches the world with confidence, yet who, when in difficulty, is disposed to turn to trusted figures for support'. This destination is contrasted with someone who is anxious and permanently in need of support and someone who never trusts anyone (Bowlby, 1973, p.209). Bowlby continues his analogy of the second model:

> In terms of this model the critical points are the junctions at which the lines fork, for once a train is on any particular line, pressures are present that keep it on that line, although, provided divergence does not become too great, there remains a chance of a train taking a convergent track when the next junction is reached (Bowlby, 1973, p. 365).

An important difference between these two models is that while in the first, setbacks result in a person becoming increasingly stuck at an early stage in development, a process that could be understood as psychologically determinist, the second takes note of the particular environment in which a person happens to be developing. This model suggests that an infinite number of variables will account for the particular pathway taken, but among those having a far reaching effect is the quality of the child's experience in his or her birth family or with alternative caregivers as well as the impact of experiences of loss or disruption of early attachment relationships. The way these are currently experienced will be reflected in current models of attachment figures and of self. These in turn will have an influence on current relationships which may increase or decrease their confidence in themselves and in the trustworthiness of particular others.

This general approach is useful when considering adolescence as a life stage along a developmental pathway which may have diverged at various points in the past from its original direction. The focus is not only on the adolescent but on environmental factors, whether immediate caregivers or factors in the wider community. This is particularly relevant to those adolescents whose circumstances make them vulnerable to suddenly losing all previous financial, practical and emotional support. Performance in the fields of work and human relations is likely to be stunted by anxiety or fear if no one is experienced as reliably available. Alternatively if previous experience has led a person to the view that no one can be relied upon other than oneself, relations at work or with friends are likely to be characterised by isolation, detachment and a failure to develop mature dependence or intimacy with anyone.

Tom's placement with the Armstrong's might be viewed, in terms of the 'branching' model as a junction where the pathway has the potential for taking a course convergent with the original. Tom rehearsed some of the more obvious junctions or critical points in his pathway prior to moving in with the Armstrongs: his separation from his sick mother and entry to the nursery, then on to foster parents. Later, there was the sudden death of his foster mother and his foster father's return to the West Indies. His foster grandmother stepped in, and her subsequent decision that she could not manage him any longer provided two more critical points for Tom. Thereafter he moved through four children's homes until he reached the Armstrong family.

Alongside this account of the junctions, Tom hints at the quality of interaction at different periods: his failure to thrive with his ill mother; his delayed speech development in the nursery; his fear of his harsh foster mother and his lack of feeling over her death; the taunting, frustration and fury between him and his foster grandmother and subsequent residential workers which escalated to repeated mutual rejection. From these we may infer a considerable degree of divergence from optimum development at different periods in Tom's developmental pathway to date. The quality of his relationship with the Armstrong's will be critical if there is to be a change for the better at this stage.

Adolescent's internal working models of self in relation to attachment figures

Different behavioural patterns of secure and insecure attachment of young children to parent figures have been recognised and classified both by empirical researchers (Ainsworth et al., 1978), clinical investigators (Bowlby, 1973), and practitioners (Fahlberg, 1981a, 1981b, 1982, 1988; Jewitt, 1982). These patterns are observable, in varying degrees, both in young children who have experienced major separations or loss of attachment figures and those that have remained in the continuous care of one or two attachment figures. Patterns of insecure attachment are characterised by manifestations of anxiety, anger, ambivalence, or detachment.

More recent empirical work by Main et al. (1985), connects individual differences in attachment to individual differences in mental representation of the self in relation to attachment figures. This reconceptualisation provides the necessary link for considering patterns of attachment in adolescents and adults. The material presented in Part 2 offers examples of characteristic patterns of attachment in a particular population of adolescents in foster care.

Attachment theory understands internal working models of self as developing from actual experiences of how significant people have behaved towards us. Models may not be wholly accessible to the person who carries them. They influence to a greater or lesser degree the way information reaches us about the people with whom we currently seek to maintain a comfortable proximity. For example, a person's internal working model of self in relation to attachment figures may distort or limit access to information as to how their attachment figures are likely to behave towards them and how they may be perceived by their attachment figures. By this means models are often actively self perpetuating.

The internal working model of an adolescent in foster care may be inferred from his or her behaviour in a number of ways:

1. *Through expectations of how significant others will behave towards him or her and how he or she expects to behave towards them.* Tom expects the Armstrongs to be furious

L goes to
dad's to provide
react? from mum.
~ anger

32

when he stays out overnight with his mother without letting them know.

2. *Through an adolescent's appraisal of situations.* This will also include the plans or programmes devised in consequence of this appraisal and the extent to which these plans may be revised, extended or checked if they appear to be redundant. Tom perceived Mr. Armstrong's requirement that he be ferried to work fourteen minutes earlier than usual one day as a form of let-down in the early days of the placement.

3. *Through an adolescent's feelings which reflect his or her appraisals.* During the afternoon that Tom missed work and plotted his revenge, there is the sense that he is struggling with strong emotion. Tom also recalled how scared he was of coming to the Armstrongs, not only because it meant moving into a totally unfamiliar situation, but because he feared they might be like his previous foster parents.

4. *Through patterns of behaviour which regulate proximity and distance between self and attachment figures.* People on an optimal pathway are able to feel comfortable in a wide range of interactions from intimacy to distance, within a significant relationship. They are able to move easily between these positions. The adolescents in the study had a much more limited and distorted range and little confidence that their foster parents would be reliably available to them when needed. This sometimes led to forms of attachment behaviour which had a quality of urgency, intensity or anger, or alternatively to behaviour which put a greater physical or emotional distance between themselves and their foster parents at the very point they were faced with a situation that threatened to overwhelm their coping capacity. This appeared to be what Tom did at the end of his placement.

5. *Through the way adolescents are able to discuss their childhood experiences in relation to their parents.* This idea will be familiar to practitioners who have worked with children or adolescents in building up a life story book. Adolescents with internal models of reliable, available attachment figures are able to convey that they value these relationships. They are able to discuss both good and bad earlier experiences with objectivity, ease and readiness of recall, an integration of

positive and negative feeling, and a lack of idealisation. Those with insecure models of attachment tend to find open emotional communication difficult, whether this is communication with their current attachment figures or about their current or earlier attachment figures. They may be dismissive of the value or significance of these relationships, appear to be cut off from the feelings associated with them, or preoccupied with dependency on their parents, lack ease of recall or display incoherence or inconsistency between their ideal and the specific memories they offer (Bretherton 1990a). Tom is entering the stage of development where he is beginning to be able to reflect on his own experience. It is from the safety of the foster home that he is able to explore his memories of childhood. In the light of new information and experience of his mother, he may be able to re-evaluate the events which led up to him coming into care.

Continuity and change

Workers with children and adolescents in care will be familiar with the fact that placement in an environment where there is sensitive, reliable care does not necessarily or automatically alter the way the young person behaves. Sometimes it seems they are set on perpetuating previous patterns of behaviour and experience, as though against their own will, even to the point of inducing their caretakers to behave uncharacteristically harshly towards them.

Tom appeared to perceive Mr Armstrong's need to give him a lift to work fourteen minutes early as either a major let-down or deliberate provocation. His reaction, which seemed out of all proportion to the event, was liable to infuriate the Armstrongs. Had they acted on this, rather than offering him straight but sympathetic feedback, it is likely that it would have perpetuated Tom's view of himself as helpless victim of unreliable and furious adults. This perception of Mr Armstrong as unreliable or provocative triggered red hot emotions of revenge in Tom which were as potentially destructive to him as to his adult carers.

Ricks seeks to integrate Bowlby's understanding of internal working models of self in relation to attachment figures with

Epstein's self-concept which emphasises the coherence of conceptual systems and the way an individual seeks to maintain this coherence 'through recreating similar experiences in subsequent attachment relationships' (Ricks, 1985, p. 213). This is important as it shifts the emphasis from the individual as passive victim of his internal working model to active participator in maintaining it intact. This seems in line with the scenario between Tom and the Armstrongs that we have just considered. This understanding accounts for continuity of behaviour and representational models, but it also provides indications for how change might come about. It is to this we now turn.

Adolescence offers special opportunities for the reorganisation of internal working models. These come about partly through the opportunities provided by increased independence for establishing significant relationships with other attachment figures outside the family. Main, following Piaget, goes further than this:

> In childhood, it is possible that internal working models of relationships can be altered only in response to changes in concrete experience. Following the onset of the stage of formal operations, it is possible that the internal working models of particular relationships established earlier can be altered. This is because these operations may permit the individual to think about thought itself, that is, to step outside a given relationship system and to see it operating (Main et al, 1985, p. 77).

In other words, through reflecting on the experience of his relationship with Mr and Mrs Armstrong, Tom may be able to revise his existing script of himself.

At the beginning of this chapter attention was drawn to the criticism, as pessimistically determinist, of theory that puts the emphasis on the influence of earlier patterns of family interaction on the adolescent. It will be seen from the argument so far that this particular formulation gives due weight to earlier experience while indicating how change might come about in the present. Tom's rapid and unhappy moves through four children's homes in the recent past might well have constituted a change for the worse along an already divergent pathway. His move to the Armstrong family might be viewed as a junction where his pathway took a

35

course more convergent with the original. Whether the equally significant junction at the end of the placement enabled him to maintain this change for the better, is more questionable.

Crossing and recrossing the family boundary: negotiations with the potential for change for adolescents in foster care

As well as developing internal working models of self in relation to attachment figures which in optimal conditions will carry the expectation of the availability and reliability of one or more preferred carers, an adolescent will also be developing parallel internal working models of self in relation to the world outside the foster family. It was argued at the beginning of this chapter that if he or she is able to experience the foster family as a secure base in the form of people he or she can rely upon to be available when needed, then confident exploration of the world outside the foster family is more likely to extend in widening circles, towards eventual mature self reliance.

Tom demonstrated this as he developed confidence at work and took considerable risks in order to get to know his mother. However it seems that he was not able to use the foster home as a secure base from which to develop friendships with his peer group, and it is doubtful whether he was able to sustain the sense of his foster family as a secure base once he left the placement.

Crossing and recrossing the boundary between the world of the family and the world outside the family is likely to have particular connotations for adolescents who have had previous painful experiences of parents and other carers leaving the house and not returning when expected or not returning at all, or themselves being removed from their families. These adolescents' internal working models are likely to have been greatly influenced as an outcome of such experiences. This in turn may be expected to influence the way they experience the negotiations between themselves and their foster parents across the family boundary.

Events, therefore that involve interaction between adolescents and their foster parents across the family boundary might be regarded as potential junctions where change might occur for better or worse, depending on whether or not old models of functioning are confirmed or challenged. Not only major events

36

like Tom returning to the Armstrong's after his unexplained absence with his mother, or the ending of the placement, but everyday events like going to work and getting back to the foster home for the evening meal could represent the critical points for reparative interaction to take place.

To summarize: in order to understand the dynamics between adolescents and their foster parents, we need to consider three things; firstly what adolescents themselves bring to their placements from the perspective of their internal working models of self in relation to attachment figures and in relation to the world outside the family; secondly the active part played by the adolescent in maintaining an existing pattern of attachment; thirdly the critical importance of negotiations between adolescent and foster parents on the boundary between the family and the world outside the foster family. This leads directly to acknowledging the importance of the way the foster family functions if an adolescent is to alter his working models of self in relation to attachment figures.

The attachment dynamic: dyadic interaction and foster family functioning

Attention needs to be given to what foster family members bring to their interaction with adolescents whom they foster. They too, carry with them working models which influence their perceptions and caregiving behaviour, and which remain more or less constant in the absence of the fostered adolescent. The impact of foster family members and adolescents on each other may be conceptualised in dyadic, interpersonal terms. Alternatively it is possible to think about the influence of the foster family as a system on the adolescent and the impact within the family system when a new adolescent member joins it.

Heard (1978, 1982) has introduced the concept of the attachment dynamic which operates within families to explain the extent to which complementary activities of attachment and caregiving behaviour govern distance regulation between family members, affect the degree in which family members engage in creative activities and influence the internal working models that each family member builds. A dynamic equilibrium between attachment, caregiving and exploratory behaviour operates in dyads such as fostered adolescent/foster parent, triads, such as the foster parent couple and the fostered adolescent and within foster family systems.

In Part 2 many of the interactional sequences which will be discussed involve an adolescent and one foster parent, even though the research interviews included the whole family whenever possible. While this method of interviewing often elicited accounts of events involving an adolescent and one foster parent, it provided less clear evidence of how foster parent couples operated together in relation to the adolescent placed with them. However some aspects of their functioning as family systems was more evident and will be discussed in Part 3.

In adolescence or adult life, attachment behaviour is aroused when a person feels anxious, upset, or is faced with a situation that they believe they cannot cope with adequately. The actual behaviour may take many forms, but the goal is always to regulate proximity to a preferred person or persons perceived as more experienced at coping with the feared situation. As the intensity of attachment behaviour rises, it overrides exploratory behaviour, which drops out. This results in effective problem solving or creative activity being discontinued until attachment behaviour has been assuaged by someone experienced as a caregiver.

Caregiving behaviour has a similar goal as attachment behaviour, that is to achieve proximity and interaction, which will enable the careseeker to cope with the situation that has triggered their attachment behaviour. Once this goal has been achieved both caregiver and careseeker are able to resume their own affairs. Heard (1982) sees exploring as finding meaning in relationships, problem solving, and constructing new internal working models of self in the world, an activity that Winnicott (1974) describes as 'play'. Heard goes on to propose that it is the operation of the attachment dynamic 'that makes it appear that individuals act together as though they constituted a more, or a less, open system' (Heard, 1982, p.101).

By focussing on the interaction between adolescent and foster parent and adolescent and foster family as a system, particularly around incidents and issues that are critical for the adolescent, it is possible to build up a picture of ways in which individual foster parents and the foster family functioning as a system, may either help or hinder the adolescent change for the better. Aspects of parental behaviour and family functioning that appear to be important in this respect are discussed in Chapters 8 and 9. Here a few key concepts are introduced.

Distance regulation

The family system needs to be flexible enough to make room for a new member. When an adolescent joins, each family member or subsystem of the family needs to be able to shift their position to some extent in response to the adolescent, rather than prescribing a slot into which the adolescent must fit. When Tom Skipper joined the Armstrong family, a good deal of the pressure to make room for him fell on the two youngest children aged 9 years and 3 years, with whom he formed intense friendships. The Armstrongs needed to be confident enough in their children's resilience to be protective but not overprotective. This family was flexible enough to let these friendships take their course and to ensure that their own children continued to have sufficient access to their parental attachment figures despite the extra demands that Tom made on their parents.

From this example it can be seen that the family also needs to tolerate a wide range of closeness and distance between its members and the fostered adolescent. The Armstrongs were flexible enough to tolerate Tom's periods of intense friendship with their young children, as well as his rather distanced behaviour from the whole family when he spent long hours on his own in his own room.

Distance regulation concerns the psychosocial distance people maintain between themselves and significant others. Byng-Hall and Campbell(1981) suggest that there are two boundaries in any relationship which regulate closeness and distance. One boundary marks the extent of comfortable intimacy, the other boundary marks the extent of comfortable distance. When attachments are secure the space between these boundaries is greater, people are able to move further apart from each other as well as enjoying closer intimacy.

The concept of distance regulation also provides a way of thinking about patterns of attachment. There are adolescents who are so anxiously attached that they cannot tolerate distance, or so detached that they shun all close relationships. Others, who behave in hostile or ambivalent ways, oscillate to and fro between closeness and distance.

Family world view, family myths and family scripts

Minuchin (1985) defines a family world view or myth as 'the shared set of conceptions by which families define themselves, their members, and the way they fit into the world.' This concept is the equivalent of the concept of internal working models within attachment theory. Certain myths, for example, that a family member's bad behaviour warrants their exclusion from the family, may result in the family not countenancing the possibility of constructive contact with members of the adolescent's birth family or of wanting to end the placement precipitately when the adolescent behaves badly. There probably needs to be a certain degree of overlap between the family myths of the foster family and the adolescent's family for the placement to be beneficial to the adolescent. However. sometimes a premature pseudomutuality develops at the beginning of a placement when both adolescent and foster family vehemently declare that the fit between them is absolute, and it is as though the adolescent has always been a member of the family. Here, the family myths which may subsequently emerge may concern anxieties about fitting in or adaptability.

Myths provide blueprints or scripts, that is, prescribed sequences of interaction triggered by particular situations. Attachment behaviour may be regarded as one form of script, exploratory interaction, however, is not scripted (Byng-Hall, 1988), and as long as family and adolescent are able together, to maintain exploratory behaviour, they may question and explore each others myths and scripts, leading to the possibility that these may change.

Open emotional communication

The ability of family members to communicate openly and with a wide range of feeling with each other about their relationships within the family and with other people significant to them is likely to enable them to engage in a similar quality of interaction with a fostered adolescent who may have more difficulies in this respect. Open communication within a family implies that the flow of interchange between subsystems, for example between the parental and sibling subsystems within the family, is not blocked. When an adolescent and foster family both have an inhibited pattern of communication, it is to be expected that the placement is less likely to be helpful to the adolescent.

Family functioning across the boundary with it's environment

The nature of the external boundary of the family system is crucial when considering styles of family functioning which are likely to be helpful to the adolescents placed with them. The boundary needs to be sufficiently permeable for the family members, fostered adolescent and other people significant to the adolescent, to pass in and out of the family with a minimum of anxiety. A family with a permeable boundary is likely to encourage contact between the adolescent and his birth family. When the boundary is permeable, adolescents are likely to be welcomed back, without fuss or angry exchanges on the threshold, in the early hours of the morning. The end of the placement will be negotiated with a view to continuity of contact, with the foster family taking their share in the initiative.

In situations likely to prove particularly difficult for the adolescent, such as going to a new school for the first time, adolescents may welcome a family member to accompany him and meet him at the end of the school day. A safe transitional zone for the adolescent is thereby established such that the adolescent is able to experience his secure base on hand while he is very anxious and unsure of himself.

Sometimes this 'holding' is extended still further, involving three way collaborative working, perhaps between a foster parent, an employer and an adolescent as in Tom Skipper's case. The analogy of the coffer dam suggested by Skynner (1974, p. 292) is useful; a coffer dam surrounds another building under construction, usually a bridge under water, protecting it until the inner building is completed and can withstand the pressure of the water.

These ideas will be discussed in more detail in Part 3, where they will be considered in relation to assessment of the foster family and the role of the social worker in building a secure base for the caregiving network.

Part 2
NEGOTIATING ACROSS
FAMILY BOUNDARIES

4 The transition to school or work

The move from an assessment centre or children's home to a foster family is usually accompanied by high hopes and dark fears; Tom Skipper hoped to escape his nightmares of the past but feared that the Armstrongs would turn out to be like his previous foster parents. No sooner has an adolescent moved into a foster family than there is likely to be another major transition to negotiate, to a new school or to work. The way foster parent and adolescent collaborate or fail to collaborate over entry to school or work at the beginning of the placement is likely to have important implications for the developing pattern of interaction between them.

Foster parents are usually highly commited to helping adolescents they foster make up for lost time in their education or get as good a start as possible at work. Despite this, it often proves difficult to anticipate the level of anxiety engendered for the adolescent at the point of entry to an unknown school or when looking for work. When anxiety is expressed in hostile or paralysed behaviour, it can be difficult to recognise the underlying fears for what they are. This chapter discusses why entry to new school or work at the beginning of the placement might be such a critical transition, it reviews some of the difficulties between adolescents and foster parents as they negotiate it and illustrates ways of working that have proved helpful to adolescents in foster care.

The concept of psychosocial transitions is concerned with

changes in our lives which take place over a relatively short space of time. The way we approach these changes is affected by our beliefs about ourselves in relation to the world we inhabit. Our experience during the transition confirms or modifies these views. These changes are lasting in their effects on us (Parkes, 1971). The transition to new school or work is approached by the majority of the adolescents in care from repeated experience of educational failure, and more generally with an internal working model of self in action in a chaotic world over which they have little control. Heard (1974), who regards Parkes' concept of a person's assumptive world as equivalent to Bowlby's concept of working models of self in action in the world, suggests that working models include models of the world and self as they might be, a probable world, an ideal world of ones desires, aspirations and goals and a dreaded world of one's worst fears. Maizels (1970), commenting on adolescent needs in the transition to school or work says:

> their problem is to find a place for themselves in this world [of adult work] which corresponds as closely as possible to their aspirations and their image of becoming adult which each individual forms for himself. (Maizels, 1970, p. 318)

One particular implication of this for adolescents in care is that they are likely to need to restructure or change the way in which they view themselves in relation to school or work. Burgess (1981), studying forty three boys in residential care, aged 15 years 9 months to 19 years 1 month, identified a pattern of educational failure characterised by truancy and instability. The brief details obtained in this study from the chronological histories of the adolescents suggest a similar pattern. Parkes (1971) identifies two components in a person's model of self in action; his capabilities, that is what he brings to a new situation, and his negotiable possessions which include the people he can turn to for help and support. Heard (1974) links this with Bowlby's understanding of the organisation of attachment behaviour in adult life and the development of goal corrected behaviour. The adolescent's model of the world and himself will influence his capacity to keep set

46

goals in mind and develop sophisticated strategies to reach them, an example would be attending school regularly or persisting with job applications on order to attain his wish to get a particular job, or a job at all. The adolescent's working models will also influence his capacity to seek and use help and support from foster parents and others over the transition.

Parkes (1971) quotes Dr Johnson in the Preface to his English Dictionary: 'Change is not made without inconvenience, even from worse to better'. At the beginning of his placement Tom Skipper said he felt unready for work; this was borne out during the first few months of part time work experience, when he arrived home exhausted and bored. It was not until he was offered a full time post, that he started to see himself and convey to others the sense that he was a working man. Like Tom, most adolescents in care have not only experienced educational failure in the past, they have faced other major, often traumatic, psychosocial transitions; coming into care and moving from place to place. The resultant 'scar tissue', to use Bowlby's analogy, is likely to be manifest in strong resistance to change. Truancy or a sense of helplessness or worthlessness may persist at a new school or there may be many absences from work despite considerable efforts to provide a better experience at this juncture. They may also continue to be reluctant to turn to their foster parents for support in the face of these difficulties.

The question arises as to the function truancy from school served for the adolescents in the study. Burgess (1981) drawing on Merton (1957) makes a useful distinction between retreatism and rebellion. With respect to retreatism, Burgess comments that it

> ...is essentially an individual response. In this sense, truancy may represent one of the most extreme forms of retreat, not just from school and its values but also from social relationships with teachers and other pupils which school represents. (Burgess, 1981, p.14).

In contrast, rebellion depends on mutual reinforcement and peer group solidarity. In the adolescents who truanted, there was little evidence of rebellion. Truancy, when it occured, seemed best understood as retreatism. Bearing this in mind, if in truanting the adolescent finds himself able to return easily to his foster family he is at least demonstrating that he does not have to turn away from all relationships.

Set against this potential resistance to change, however, the theory would also lead us to expect a greater susceptibility to influence for a time limited period around the transition. Heard (1974) comments, 'attachment behaviour is aroused when the probable world comes near the dreaded world'. We need to be able to turn to people that we can trust when we think our worst fears are about to be realised. This must have been Tom's experience when, at the beginning of his placement, it looked as though he was going to be early for work. Even if he could not always meet Tom's demands, Mr Armstrong's recognition of the way Tom expressed his anxiety about work was a critical factor in the development of an alliance between them. As the placement developed, Tom continued to turn to Mr Armstrong for support, when necessary.

This links with the 'branchline' model of development discussed in Chapter 3. The transition into the placement and then almost immediately the process of negotiating entry to new school or work could be regarded as a junction which carries the potential for an adolescent's pathway to shift for better or worse. In approximately one third of the placements in the study, foster parents were able to recognise and respond appropriately to adolescents' anxiety around this transition, and were successful in forming an alliance which continued to be a constructive influence within the placement. These placements lasted between seven and twenty six months, which was usually about the time they had been planned for, only two ended in disruption. In contrast, in another one third of the placements, foster parents missed or misunderstood the cues they were being offered, usually because anxiety was not expressed directly. The prognosis for these placements was poor. The placements for this group lasted between three months and seven months, less than the time that had been planned for them. For the remaining one third of placements a less clear picture emerged. These were the ones where entry to school, college or work was welcomed. or at least did not appear to arouse a great deal of anxiety. For these, whether alliances formed early in the placement or not, seemed to depend on other factors. Placements lasted between four months and twenty six months.

Case Studies

In the following detailed accounts of five adolescents, two were moving from 'inside' schools attached to the residential institutions where they had been living, three were looking for jobs. The focus is on the negotiations between them and their foster parents.

Dawn Gibson

After three years at 'inside' schools in an assessment centre and a community home with education on the premises, entry to a new 'outside' school was anticipated with great apprehension by Dawn aged 15 years. Her foster mother commented:

> ...she wouldn't go to school on her own, I took her up to school on the first morning – oh, I wasn't going to take her to school on the first morning – and she begged and pleaded with me to take her, and although she'd been round the school, she knew where the school was, and she was very, very hesitant when I left her at the school, and um, then she wanted me to go and meet her in the evening as well from the school, you know...

Dawn expressed her anxiety directly, in the form of a request for her foster mother to accompany her. Mrs Hatton did not get alarmed that this was not 'age-appropriate' behaviour or that if she met Dawn's request she would be encouraging over dependency. Dawn's attachment behaviour was assuaged by Mrs Hatton's response, and she was soon able to go to school on her own.

Frank Little

Frank was aged 16 years 9 months when his placement started, he had had all his education in a residential special school. His reaction to the prospect of finding work was one of paralysis, for the first month he would hardly leave his foster home for any reason:

Mrs Murphy	...Frank found it very difficult to go looking for work, to actually ask to go for interviews, he found that very hard indeed...in the end I threw him out, if you like.
Interviewer	How do you mean, you threw him out? He's still here.
Mrs Murphy	...I cajoled, I asked, I offered, I gave him lists, I made millions of telephone calls on his behalf, trying to fix things up and Frank sat for four weeks and made no effort whatsoever and would not even go out of the door to go try any of these places that I'd rung round...So, after four weeks, I had a word with the social worker and said, 'Well I'm putting my foot down'; so we devised a plan...I simply made Frank go out of the house at half past eight in the morning and he was allowed to return home for lunch and then he went out again...

Frank's immobility might be understood as a form of 'frozen behaviour' in the face of overwhelming fear (Bowlby, 1973, p. 90) Alternatively it might be viewed as straightforward laziness, or again as a recognition at some level of his unreadiness for work and wish to regress to total dependency on his foster family. Yet he seemed unable to use their efforts on his behalf. All three explanations have common threads of Frank's avoidance of launching out into the unknown and taking risks, his inability to use the help offered by his foster parents and his inability to tell them directly what would help.

The Murphy's strategy worked to the extent that, with the help of further phone calls between Mrs Murphy and the careers office, Frank embarked on a work experience programme. He never gave his foster parents any feedback about this, keeping the two worlds of work and foster home quite separate. Frank never showed much evidence of drawing on his foster parents' help or resources and the placement never really got off the ground. After five months the placement ended at the foster parents request, as they felt they were not achieving anything with Frank.

The Muphy's failure to form an alliance with Frank raises the question of what course of action might have been effective.

Frank's experience of institutionalisation appeared to have left him severely incapacitated in using help or expressing directly what he needed. Our understanding of psychosocial transitions leads us to expect a time limited period at the beginning of the placement when Frank would be most open to influence (Parkes,1971; Heard, 1974.) Perhaps leaving Frank for a month before any radical steps were taken contributed to his paralysis. In the study, most instances of successful alliance formation around the transition to school or work involved the foster parents in accompanying the adolescent for at least some of their early, critical journeys to school, to the careers office or to employers' doors when they went for job interviews. The problem was not that this engendered prolonged dependency in the adolescents; on the contrary, once their anxiety had been recognised and responded to, they managed reasonably well themselves. Rather, the difficulties for foster parents were in finding ways of making an offer to accompany that was acceptable to the adolescent, and then staying tuned in to their indirect, sometimes distorted expressions of anxiety. In the next two examples, foster parents appeared to miss critical signals.

Gina Fitzgerald

The transition for Gina Fitzgerald, aged 15 years 8 months, involved returning after a four month stay in an Assessment Centre with an 'inside' school to the school she had attended in the past and from which she had persistently truanted. It was not so much Gina's anxiety as her insolence that Mrs Henderson reported:

> ...this was really the first time I saw Gina in a different light. We went into the headmistress's room and she...said ' Now Gina, are you going to try?' 'Course I am!' and this sort of sharp...um...insolent to the headmistress, but never to me, you know, up to this time,...but the headmistress obviously knew her, and accepted her back and said that she would keep in touch if Gina ran away. She had a little chat with me.

Not only does Gina have difficulty in conveying her anxiety, but her foster mother loses an opportunity to establish an alliance with Gina through recognising the panic behind the insolence. The only working relationship that gets established appears to be between Mrs Henderson and the headmistress, around their concern that Gina might continue to truant. Gina probably experienced this as an alliance formed against her. Contrast this with Tom Skipper, where the beginnings of an alliance was first established between Tom and Mr Armstrong and then the working relationship between Mr Armstrong and Mr Thackwray, Tom's employer, 'held' Tom through the initial difficult weeks in the job.

Christine Faber

With Christine, aged 16 years, the cue was different again. Mrs Hatton describes accompanying Christine to the careers office:

Mrs Hatton	She'd go down to the Careers and...she wouldn't go by herself, I had to go with her, if I went with her she was fine and anything on the board she'd just look at it and she'd say, 'Look, I'm going to take it. I don't care what it is now. OK, I'll even take a YOPS thing...because I want to get out'...And then she got short listed...to two jobs with the opportunity to go to college as well. She was absolutely positive she'd got these jobs, and she didn't get them and that really upset her. She was really upset over them and said...that was it. 'Aren't going to try any more.'
Interviewer	Did she...have any idea why the other girls got it in each case or not?
Mrs Hatton	Well because of the schooling. They ...got good school reports.
Interviewer	Was she told that or is it just what she...?
Mrs Hatton	Well yes. One of the girls and one of the men that interviewed her...made a comment about why didn't she go to school?...she brooded and she was saying, 'It's not fair'...She was saying she'd come into care and,..she couldn't get a job and I said...'being in care's nothing whatsoever to do

with it.' Because everyone knew, you know, you put your address down and say you live with an aunt, you know, so you haven't to say you're in care or anything, that's got nothing whatsoever to do with it.

Probably both explanations held some truth. Mrs Hatton failed to recognise with Christine, the way in which her sense of stigma at being in care was affecting her approach to finding a job. Immediately after these incidents Christine absconded and found work for herself. Although their alliance had not been strong enough to prevent Christine's flight, it was sufficient for her to maintain contact with Mrs Hatton by phone, while concealing where she was living. The story of this placement will be continued in Chapter 6.

Andy West

Andy, aged 16 years 6 months had very clear goals; he wished to be a success in the same trade as his father. His plans to acheive these goals by becoming a motor mechanic, had been disastrously thwarted in the recent past, first by being sacked by the foreman of his father's firm for being drunk at work, and subsequently from another similar firm for frenetic, chaotic, careless work. He could see only too clearly how these experiences had contributed to his rapid detioration and high risk of custodial sentence for repeatedly drinking and driving under age. He had an extremely high investment in finding work.

Initially he had to face a series of setbacks. He was twice turned down for a work experience scheme on the grounds that his prospective employers 'didn't take to the lad'. One specifically linked his decision with Andy having been 'sacked by his father'. Andy and his foster father recalled the frustrations they experienced with a slow moving careers officer:

Mr Armstrong   But anyhow she came into...where we were and she stood there and I thought, 'is she going to say something?' And...

Andy   She looked at us, idle, and then walked in office!

Mr Armstrong   And then she came back and I said, 'what's

	happening then?' She said, 'What? What?' and I said, 'Well what's happening about a garage?' She said, 'Oh yes' she said, 'Can't seem to find one, can we?'
Andy	We've run out!
Mr Armstrong	And I said, 'So what are you going to do then?' I said 'He could have had a proper...an ordinary job two weeks ago if we'd known!...Can't you just prepare...' She said, I've done the preparation, I've prepared them for you!' I felt like saying well you haven't done it blooming well then!...We stalked out of the place and we went down the town, 'Ah, there's a garage round the back of here' and I rushed round there, I said 'Stay there a minute, don't come with me!' No that wasn't the reason actually! And I raced round there 'cos Harry had taken his car there some months ago and I was very impressed by them actually, don't often get impressed by garages! And I rushed around there and told the chap the story and he'd never heard of the scheme or anything, anyhow...he's actually considering it and I rushed back to the Youth Employment again to see this silly woman and said 'I think we've got a garage! But would you please ask Miss So-and-so to ring him up because he wants to know a bit more about it?'

Mr Armstrong accompanies Andy to the careers office and experiences the frustrations at first hand. His reactions could hardly be described as professional in the sense of detached collaboration with fellow professionals. They seem more like those of a parent fighting for a job for his son! He is clear that time is of the essence if Andy's worst fears about himself are not to overwhelm him with despair.

Andy returns to the threat these job interviews held for him.

Andy	I don't know what it is that people don't like about me.
Mr Armstrong	Well...he was a funny old codger anyway, wasn't

	he? The first one.
Andy	And the second one were a right weird...
Mr Armstrong	Well, I mean, I didn't like the sound of either of them...I think this fella, he's only young, he's only about 33 or 4 himself...
Andy	Well, my other boss, I got on brilliant with him. He bought me a sheepskin coat. He took me out to pubs on dinner times and that for a snack and what have you.
Mr Armstrong	That was half the trouble, wasn't it, the last time? Didn't you have a few too many pints?
Andy	Well, all kinds of, well, it were actually foreman what sacked me. It wasn't John. It were foreman...
Mr Armstrong	Yes.
Andy	....who disliked me.
Mr Armstrong	You see, the trouble is there are too many people chasing too few jobs, so why employ someone that they don't really take to? They shouldn't, should they really, someone'll come along who they do take to, that's more or less what the first chap said, so I mean, you know, you've just got to hope that the next bloke does say 'He seems alright'. I mean he hasn't got to take to you, he's just got to think, 'Oh, I think he'll be alright.'

Andy is in danger of shifting to a global evaluation of himself as unlikeable, in line with his dreaded model of self in relation to the world. Mr Armstrong responds by reformulating what has happened into a number of different issues: whether Andy would really have wanted to work for the first two employers: the real reason he was sacked before was not dislikeability but drink, the competition for jobs and the need for Andy to demonstrate competance. He was able to do this far more effectively for having been in the thick of the experience with Andy, and indeed it is unlikely that Andy would have sustained his search for work without Mr Armstrong's reassuring presence and intervention. Andy still has to make the running himself in the job interviews but he has received potent reinforcement towards a changed view of himself. He is able to approach the next interview as a potentially competent worker who was having to contend with competition and a poor work record, rather than as totally and irretrievably unlikeable. Andy was successful in getting this third job.

Implications for practice

This final section summarizes the processes of intervention that appear to be helpful to adolescents around the transition to school or work at the beginning of the placement.

Timing may be crucial; many adolescents are extremely anxious about managing this move successfully and, at the same time, may be open to help for a time limited period. Mr Armstrong's intervention with Andy West provides a good example of what this might involve and it may have actually prevented the placement disrupting. The same may have been true with Tom Skipper. Perhaps leaving Frank Little for a month before any radical steps were taken contributed to his paralysis.

Behaviour aimed at gaining and retaining proximity to someone perceived as stronger and wiser is likely to be aroused when adolescents believe that their worst fears are about to be realised. Until this attachment behaviour is assuaged, they will be unable to function to the best of their ability. Many of those who received an inadequate or unreliable response to their attachment behaviour in infancy and childhood, are likely to find it hard to ask for help directly; their requests may be hidden in hostility, as with Gina Fitzgerald or paralysis, as with Frank Little. Christine Faber's attachment behaviour was inhibited by her sense of stigma at being in care. When this was not acknowledged and instead she was confronted by her previous failures, she took flight, confirming a developing pattern of compulsive self reliance. Foster parents need to pay close attention to direct and distorted requests for help and be ready to respond. Provided it is the adolescents' attachment behaviour that is held in focus and assuaged, rather than foster parents' needs to overprotect, then a prolonged period of overdependency is unlikely.

With the placements in the research study, formation of an alliance around the common objective of the adolescent re-entering 'outside' school or finding work was associated with mutually satisfying placements which ran their planned course. Failure to form an alliance at this point might be regarded as a warning sign that all is not well. This seems to be the case particularly when the adolescent is lacking in self reliance and has a history of school failure and avoidance of difficulties.

Intervention at the appropriate time and distance is insufficient unless the adolescent is convinced that their foster parents are on their side. Gina Fizgerald, and Christine Faber and Frank Little were not sure of this. In contrast, Andy West, within a strong alliance, was able to name and explore his fear of being generally dislikeable, and Mr Armstrong was able to provide feedback in the form of evidence from their experiences together that Andy's model of self in the world was inaccurate.

Some adolescents, from the start of the placement, are sufficiently sustained by their experience of their foster family as a secure base, that they could manage to get to school or find jobs on their own. However, all those discussed so far needed one of their foster parents to move across the family boundary with them, to be on hand to provide a secure base outside the family home. For this alliance to be effective, the foster parent does not share the adolescent's worst fears, so is available both to support and to teach coping skills. Together, they establish a safe transitional zone outside the family home in which to face a world which the adolescent would otherwise experience as hostile or overwhelming.

The capacity of a foster family to form a safe transitional zone for an adolescent will depend on the permeability of the family boundary. This is because foster parents need to feel at ease moving out with the adolescent into an uncertain and possibly frustrating situation.

At the same time as maintaining a strong alliance with an adolescent, a foster parent may be needing to establish other coalitions with teachers, careers officers or employers. The analogy of the coffer dam, introduced in Chapter 3, is useful to describe effective three-way working outside the foster home. This failed with Gina Fizgerald because instead of being contained within the working relationship between her foster mother and head teacher, she was left on the outside of their alliance. It succeeded with Tom Skipper and Andy West, who were both held through the early stages of their entry to work within the coffer dam established by Mr Armstrong and their employers.

As with the formation of safe transitional zones, a foster family's capacity for establishing coffer dams will be partly dependent on the permeability of the family boundary. It will also depend on the family's capacity and skill in forming an alliance with the adolescent, as this needs to precede coalitions between foster parents and other adults. This argues for a reallocation of roles between social workers and foster parents such that foster parents take responsibility for helping the adolescent negotiate this transition. A further argument for this is that many adolescents require an intensity of psychological support over this period that cannot usually be offered by a generic social worker or a careers officer.

5 Interaction between fostered adolescents, their birth families and their foster parents

Most of the adolescents in the study were in frequent contact with at least one relative or previous carer. This chapter describes some of the adolescents' main preoccupations in relation to their birth families and discusses how these affected them and their foster parents and the relationship between them. It explores ways in which foster parents' approach either helps or hinders adolescents to come to a more realistic appraisal of their families.

Twenty of the adolescents in the study were in contact with one or more relative or previous carer at least monthly through the placement. For many, contact was considerably more frequent and only three adolescents had no contact with either of their birth parents. This is similar to the picture that emerges in the Kent Family Project (Yelloly, 1979; Smith, 1986).

The adolescents in the study were typically members of large families; out of twenty two, seventeen were from families of four or more children, sixteen were middle children. Twenty were in contact with siblings and eight with grandparents. While they could not avoid meeting their parents' new partners on their visits home, of the eight adolescents who mentioned or discussed step-parents, in only one case were they presented in a favourable light.

The adolescents had two main preoccupations in relation to these contacts. Firstly they were concerned with exploring and coming to terms with their feelings about their family. Following experiences of family disruption, rejection and separation most adolescents started their placements with an image of their parents or other previous caregivers as monstrous or ideal. In order to unlink themselves from an obsolete internal working model of self in relation to an attachment figure, they needed to become as fully aware as possible of their more complex feelings for the real person behind the image. Secondly, they were preoccupied with testing out their birth family's current and future reliability; this was particularly linked to their need to find a home base for themselves when the time limited placement ended and they left care.

Adolescents in time limited placements differ from younger foster children or from adolescents placed on a permanent basis in two important respects. Firstly, they have a very much larger element of choice and control about contact with their parents than is likely to be the case for younger children. Adolescents are able to travel increasingly long distances unaccompanied. They need no longer be at the mercy of parents visiting or failing to visit them or of agency policy or decisions about contact. They are also more likely to be able to seek out lost relatives without recourse to their social workers; for example, one enterprising girl sought and found her father after her mother's death by ringing up all the numbers under his name until a woman who answered put the phone down on her when she explained why she was ringing. Secondly, unlike most adolescents placed on a permanent basis, they are preoccupied with finding a reliable home base for themselves as an insurance against the day when the time limited placement ends and/or they leave care.

Any evaluation of the quality of adolescents' contact with their parents or the wisdom of their wish to return home is, of course, a highly complex matter. In most cases the principle put forward by Fanshel and Shinn (1978), that it makes for better adjustment to be in contact with a flawed parent than be coping with fantasies about an absent parent, is likely to hold good for adolescents in time limited foster care. This was also the evidence of the research on which Holman (1975, 1980) based his model of inclusive fostering, a model which encompasses not only face to face contact between child and parent but an inclusive attitude and approach on the part of the foster parents.

It may be harder to come to terms with real parents in their absence, but contact does not automatically result in a realistic perception of parents. There were several instances in the study where an adolescent might be in face to face contact with a parent and yet maintain an idealised view of them despite strong current evidence presented through the parents' behaviour towards them. Similarly, there was no evidence that a decision to return home was necessarily linked with resolution of feelings towards birth parents. Economic necessity, sheer loneliness, or desperation of finding anyone else to provide a bed when a placement disrupted were powerful shaping events associated with return home.

One implication of adolescents' increased choice and control over contact with parents and their preoccupation with finding a home base for the future is that they are liable to take considerable risks for themselves. There are the risks involved in discovering about the past. For some, this will include choices and decisions about whether to seek out 'missing' or 'lost' parents who, as in Tom Skipper's case, may turn out to be mentally ill or vagrants or in other respects far from their idealised parent figure. They must risk the possibility of having their fears confirmed that it was they who were responsible for destroying or disrupting their family or causing the illness or death of a family member. There are other risks for the present and the future: if they test out their families now, will they find them still unable to care or that family life has moved on and the family circle has closed, firmly excluding them? When this happens, will they be able to sustain the disillusionment of their hopes of an ideal re-formed home without succumbing to suicidal depression or serious disruptive, delinquent behaviour?

If adolescents are pushing themselves almost to their limits in risk taking, some difficult or disturbed behaviour and affect is to be expected, and this is apparent in two of the case studies that follow.

Case Studies

The three detailed case studies in this chapter are representative of three groups which emerged in the study. These groups are based on an association between the family members or previous significant carers with whom the adolescent had most frequent contact in the course of the placement, the size of their birth or early reconstituted families, the age they came into care, and who the adolescent went to live with at the end of the placement.

Group 1

Ten adolescents were most frequently in touch with one or both birth parents. They tended to be from smaller families than the others, most had younger siblings at home or with relatives. This group were 10 years old or over when they came into care. Six went to live with birth parents at the end of the placement or soon after. The case study of Andy West placed with the Armstrongs comes from this group.

Group 2

Six adolescents were most frequently in contact with one or more older siblings living independently. They were all members of families with four or more children with at least two older siblings. They all came into care under the age of 13 years. When the placement ended two went to live with older siblings and one with birth parents. The case study of Ben Little placed with the Wilkinsons comes from this group.

Group 3

Six adolescents were most frequently in touch with a range of significant carers, either grandparents or non-related carers. Four were from families with five or more children. Like Group 2 they all came into care under the age of 13 years. When the placement ended two had periods living with previous carers, but four out of this group moved rapidly through a succession of living arrangements which included a higher proportion of places provided statutorily than the other two groups. The case study of Mandy Shepperd placed with Mrs Hatton comes from this group.

In the first group there appears to be a relationship between spending a longer period of time at home before coming into care, maintaining most frequent contact with birth parents and returning to live at home subsequently. In the second group where the most frequent contact was with an older sibling it is possible that older brothers and sisters in large families might have become significant carers to the adolescents now in foster care, either while they were all still living at home or when they moved together into residential care. In the third group grandparents appeared to have played a very significant part in the care of adolescents in six cases. Some grandparents had offered concurrent care to that being given by parents, others had taken over care when parents left home or died. The only two significant non-related carers with whom adolescents had most frequent contact were both from previous foster families.

The case studies of Andy West, Ben Little and Mandy Shepperd are presented within a similar structure. A brief history is followed by a summary of the pattern of contact between adolescent and birth family and other previous carers through the placement. The adolescent's perception of the purpose of the placement in relation to these contacts, is identified. Illustrations of the interaction between adolescent, foster parents and birth parents and others is used to demonstrate the foster parents' perceptions of these contacts and helpful and unhelpful approaches by foster parents.

In the final section of this chapter, common factors and key issues are identified which appear to help or hinder adolescents reappraise their family relationships and test them out as a possible home base for the future.

Andy West

Andy was the third child in a family of four children, the only one in his family not living with a parent. He was commited to care when he was 15 years 10 months. His court appearances for drinking and driving under age had started three years earlier around the time his father received a custodial sentence. His parents divorced and when his father came out of prison Andy was passed to and fro between them and their new partners, while his behaviour continued to deteriorate. Eventually both sides of the family regarded his behaviour as beyond their control. His placement with the Armstrong family started when he was 16 years 6 months and lasted for fifteen months.

At the start of the placement, Andy was in contact with his parents and paternal grandparents at least monthly by phone, letter or visits to them. When he was approaching a critical court appearance for driving under age, contact became more frequent, almost daily. He would drive, illegally, up to forty five miles to see his mother. After this crisis, his feelings and pattern of contact appeared to shift towards more warmth and contact with his mother and increasing hostility and less contact with his father. His relations with his grandparents remained consistent, with increased contact if they were ill when he helped to care for them.

Andy saw the purpose of the placement as 'time for me to forgive them and them to forgive me'. Initially he hoped that after a year he would return to live with his father, but when the placement ended after fifteen months he went to live with his mother and her new partner.

Initially, Andy took to heart his father's wish that 'he would sort himself out'. He was concerned to gain his father's approval by demonstrating his business skills in the same trade. He claimed 'if I'm really good, Dad will get me a new car', Mr Armstrong responded: 'that sounds like a bribe' and '"behave" is a bad sort of word, all you need to do is grow up'. In doing this Mr Armstrong reframed Andy's agenda and went on to offer a more positive reconstruction of his father's bribe; 'Dad wanted Andy to do well'. He also reinforced Andy's positive sense of family identity: 'Andy has the knack of buying and selling, it runs in the family'.

As Andy approached the crisis of the critical court hearing, he recalled the time when, furious with his father, he had driven his father's car into a wall. He was angry again now over his father's neglect of him in this crisis; his father cared only for himself. Again, Mr Armstrong offered a more positive construction; Andy's father was upset because he wanted to be proud of his son, but was reminded of his bad behaviour.

Three months later, however, Mr Armstrong was acknowledging that although Andy's father came over to the foster home several times around the court hearing, 'he makes promises and doesn't keep them'. Andy wanted Mr Armstrong to talk with his father about his neglect. Mr Armstrong responded by writing to Mr West to invite him to a planning meeting on Andy's future. A year into the placement Mr West attended the planning meeting and promised to look for a job and accommodation for Andy near home. He appeared to take no action subsequently and Mr Armstrong agreed with Andy that his father had let him down.

Andy's disillusionment and despair at his father's failure to take any action on his behalf overshadowed the last weeks of the placement; Mrs Armstrong commented: 'Andy was near suicidal because his Dad was taking no notice.' Yet the Armstrongs regarded Andy's threat to be 'rotten' to his father in retaliation as childish and ineffective; they advised: 'you ought to stay friends with dad, you may need him.'

In contrast to Andy's idealisation of his father at the start of the placement, he had no time for his mother, perhaps he could not bear to acknowledge her concern for him. 'I can't read Mum's letters.....she's 45 miles away'. When Andy explained his illegal driving in terms of his need to be with his mother when he was worrying about his imminent court appearance, Mrs Armstrong was mildly cynical about this 'excuse'. However contact between the Armstrongs and Andy's mother was consolidated when she phoned them to alert them to Andy's illegal driving. Andy was both furious and relieved and appeared to become more law abiding, at least for a period, after this.

The Armstrongs met Andy's paternal grandfather more than once, and were well aware of how fond of he and Andy were of each other. After Andy's grandfather had a heart attack while Andy was staying there, Andy said 'don't blame it on me.' Mr Armstrong responded 'it never entered my head', and went on to explain that Andy had spent a week of his holiday looking after his grandfather. They recognised Andy's distress when his hopes of a home with his grandparents were dashed as their health deteriorated. By the end of the placement Andy's grandmother had had several heart attacks too, but Andy was able to celebrate her survival; 'she's as strong as an ox.'

At the start of the placement the Armstrongs concentrated on being in touch with Andy's preoccupations about whether there would be a home for him with his father or grandparents when the placement ended but stressed that he must work within the timing and pacing offered by the placement. Keeping in step with Andy, Mr Armstrong reflected back Andy's wish to regain his father's approval, pointed to evidence of his parents' feelings for him. He joined in Andy's project to test out his father's commitment to Andy by writing to Mr West and monitoring his response. As Andy increasingly drew attention to evidence of his father's lack of concern, Mr Armstrong confirmed this perception, never criticising Andy's anger, but shifting to encourage Andy to accept his family as they are, with all their flaws and limitations. The

Armstrongs welcomed contact and collaboration with all members of Andy's family.

Ben Little

Ben was the fourth child in a family of six children. He was committed to care with his brothers via a Place of Safety Order when he was 2 years 3 months. At the same time his parents were convicted of neglect and imprisoned for six months. When his parents came out of prison, Ben returned home for two and a half years, he returned to care at the age of 5 years when his mother left home. Ben spent the next eight years at a large residential school for educationally subnormal children, three of his older brothers were placed with him. Holidays were spent in three different children's homes, and eventually, regularly in one to which they all moved when Ben was 14 years. His placement with the Wilkinson family lasted twenty six months, starting when he was 15 years.

On one occasion Ben and one of his older brothers travelled fifty miles by train back to the residential school to visit a member of the domestic staff who had kept in correspondence with them. They planned another visit but she died unexpectedly before it happened.

At the start of the placement Ben visited his birth father and stepmother fortnightly. The gap between visits widened, largely, because visiting was actively discouraged by his stepmother. Ben had had no contact with his mother for years.

Contact with his three older brothers, no longer in care, developed and feelings diversified and strengthened as they quarrelled and shifted in their alliances. Ben remained consistent in his wish to share a flat with one particular brother. In contrast, his contact with a slightly older brother and younger sister who were still in care was unspontaneous, the visits being 'arranged' and 'encouraged' by their social worker and foster parents. Ben's feelings for these two remained neutral and distanced.

Ben appeared to use the placement to renew his contact with his older brothers and stepbrothers. Testing out the possibility of returning to live with father and stepmother remained secondary to establishing how reliable his brothers were likely to be. The brothers appeared to operate their own agenda regarding visits to their father and stepmother's home and used Ben's foster home as a meeting place for their operations.

Mr and Mrs Wilkinson visited Ben's father and stepmother once at the start of the placement. They subsequently commented that they saw no point in contact with parents; 'it is not our place to advise or judge or presume'. They saw this as the social worker's role.

During the first research interview, the Wilkinsons made few references to Ben's past life other than the childrens home he had just left. Ben, however, spoke with warmth about his residential school, saying it was the place he thought of as home. It seemed nobody had heard this before, or could imagine how such a large institution could be thought of as 'home'. Ben's older brothers were hardly mentioned. In later interviews it was left to the researcher to ask specific questions about Ben's contact with his family, and these questions seemed to give Ben permission to talk about his family in the presence of his foster parents.

The Wilkinson's attitude to Ben's older brothers was mixed, they did a great deal to arrange for Ben and his favourite brother to have a holiday together. However, they also perceived Ben's brothers as a bad influence on him, and likely to exploit him. The fact that the brothers were not working was cited as evidence for this, and they were concerned that Ben's brothers had persuaded Ben to give them money, clothes and other possessions which could be sold for cash. The Wilkinsons' warnings to Ben against his brothers became increasingly anxious and sermonic as the placement neared its end, coupled with criticism of Ben's carelessness in allowing himself to be thus exploited. Ben seemed reasonably content with his relationships with his brothers and stuck out against the combined plans of his social worker and foster parents to find him lodgings on his own. He eventually gained their reluctant agreement that he move into a semi-independent living unit with his brothers.

The Wilkinsons had a clear agenda of their own, linked with their quite understandable wish to see Ben develop into a respectable citizen. Their agenda was to discourage Ben's close contact with his three older brothers and to encourage his contact with his brother and sister still in care. In neither case did their attitudes or intervention appear to shift Ben's perception or agenda, but it probably inhibited him from sharing what he really felt about them with his foster parents. Their difficulties in staying in touch with Ben's preoccupations and agenda, and in confining themselves to straight feedback on the consequences of his behaviour in relation to his brothers probably hindered Ben in reappraising his relationships with his family. They had little confidence that by attending to Ben's concerns, he might in time learn to form his own judgements.

Mandy Shepperd

Mandy was the second child in a family of six children. None were brought up by their mother who gave Mandy as a baby to a friend, Mrs Samuel. Mrs Samuel had a large family by several men. Mandy remained on an unregistered private fostering arrangement with this turbulent family until she was 12 years old. During this period Mrs Samuel was admitted to psychiatric hospital several times. The 'placement' ended with reception into care when Mandy and Mrs Samuel were charged with shoplifting. In a violent argument Mrs Samuel disowned Mandy as her daughter. When Mandy visited her from the children's home at 13 years of age, Mrs Samuel threatened to commit suicide in front of her

At 14 years of age Mandy was placed with foster parents, the Martin's. After a year when she stole from them, they asked for her to be removed and she returned to the children's home. During her last year at school, Mandy developed an important relationship with a woman teacher and this continued after she left school; Mandy valued the privacy this relationship afforded her, as she trusted the teacher not to pass on her confidences to the statutory caregiving network.

Mandy's placement with Mrs Hatton lasted twenty five months, starting when she was 16 years of age. For the first six months of the placement Mandy explored the possibility of having a home base again with Mrs Samuel. This culminated in a dramatic and bitter confrontation between Mandy, Mrs Samuel and some of Mrs Samuel's children. Mandy broke off contact with the Samuel family and for the next ten months focussed her attention on her birth mother whom she could not remember. She engaged in regular information seeking and reflective sessions with her social worker and eventually decided that she did not want to request a meeting with her mother. In the last few months of the placement Mandy turned towards her more recent foster family, the Martins. The renewed contact flourished over the transition to independent living and Mandy subsequently spent a period of several months living with this family.

While not stating purposes explicitly, Mandy appeared to use the placement to explore her feelings for her mother and previous foster parents and to test out her previous foster parents' reliability as providers of a future home base. She seemed to do this sequentially, rather than in parallel.

Mrs Hatton encouraged Mandy's efforts to keep in contact with Mrs Samuel, putting a positive construction on Mandy's behaviour; 'Mandy is really caring' and emphasising that Mrs Samuel was a sick woman who needed care. However she also made it clear that she did not want Mrs Samuel creating a scene at the foster home, as had happened elsewhere in the past, and she kept her at arms length through phone contact. This period culminated in one of Mrs Samuel's sons coming looking for her and 'kidnapping' her for a family meeting where Mandy was accused of being the cause of the family breakup, and was told by Mrs Samuel: 'go back on the streets with your prostitute mother, that's all you're good for.'

When Mrs Hatton became anxious about Mandy's absence and asked the police to look for her, their intervention precipitated Mrs Samuel into threats of murder and suicide. After this, Mrs Hatton wished to limit but not prevent this contact, but Mandy decided to stop visiting Mrs Samuel: 'I can't help her, perhaps I can help my Mum'.

Mandy worked regularly with her social worker to this end and ten months later saw her full birth certificate for the first time. During this period she commented;

> I just want to see one person of my whole family, so I can say, you know,....I have got people and I have seen who they are. Whereas you can't before, and it seems silly to say to the college students that you haven't got a Mum and Dad because you've never seen them before, and then they're sort of asking questions, well why?...I wouldn't

force her but I would like to know, you know, what has happened, and I think when I was younger – say about thirteen...I could have killed my Mum and Dad then. But now I think I've got a bit more mature...I could just sit there...it might be a shock...

Later, at a critical point near the end of the placement, when Mandy was engaged in a stormy encounter with the police who were accusing her of soliciting, a policeman attempted to divert her anger by pointing out an attractive plain-clothes policewoman. Mandy immediately took her to be her mother: 'its my mother, Its my mother, I'm a pro, Mum's a pro, C's [Mrs Samuel] a pro.' By the end of the placement Mandy's wish to meet her birth mother appeared to have faded.

During this period Mrs Hatton remained anxiously in the background, concerned to support Mandy in her efforts to come to terms with her birth mother, but fearful of the psychological stress this was placing on Mandy. Although Mandy and Mrs Hatton had fallen out with the previous statutory foster parents, the Martins, at the beginning of the placement, Mandy gradually reapproached them. By this time Mandy was feeling less sure how long she could stay with Mrs Hatton, who was unwell. This time, when the storm broke, the lines were drawn differently, with Mandy and her social worker siding against Mrs Hatton. Mrs Hatton subsequently commented about this incident that she was

so angry, they'd [the Martin's] only had Mandy a few months because she'd started stealing from them when she was thirteen or fourteen and they wanted her out straight away.

It may be easier for a foster parent to forgive limited parenting by birth parents or their friends than that offered by other statutory foster parents. The relationship between Mandy and the Martins flourished at a highly idealised level over Mandy's transition to independent living. After a few months, Mandy moved into the Martin's home for about a year.

Mrs Hatton's responses to Mandy's efforts to test out her feelings for Mrs Samuel and her birth mother were sensitively balanced between encouragement and protection. Her wish to protect Mandy was particularly acute at times when she felt Mandy was at considerable risk, either from external factors such as venturing into the red light district to visit Mrs Samuel, or from inner stress as instanced in Mandy's apparently tenuous hold on reality when confronted by the police with allegations of her prostitution. In contrast to the way she was able to tune into Mandy's agenda in these first two ventures, her interventions in relation to Mandy's previous statutory foster parents were frankly antagonistic. The Martins appeared to be regarded as unwelcome rivals, and Mandy's efforts to reestablish herself with them as 'manipulative'. This did not deter Mandy, indeed it may have had the opposite effect, but the relationship appeared to stick at rather an idealised level, unlike the more realistic resolution she appeared to acheive in relation to Mrs Samuel and her birth mother.

Implications for practice

In this final section I shall draw the threads together by considering the main implications for practice for foster parents and social workers. At the start of this chapter it was argued that adolescents in time limited foster care are usually engaged in two psychosocial tasks in relation to their birth families and other previous caregivers, which involve reappraising these relationships and testing out their reliability as a home base for the future. They have considerable freedom to pursue this agenda which often seems to be experienced as so urgent that it necessitates taking considerable external and internal risks. It is as though they engage in a series of pilot projects in pursuing these two main tasks. These pilot projects may be formulated speculatively by the adolescent, but not shared explicitly with anyone else at the time. Some may be tested out, others such as Mandy's plan to meet her birth mother, may be rejected after reflection.

The foster family as a secure base for exploration and risk taking

It is useful to think of the adolescent's foster family as having the potential to offer a secure base for their explorations, whether these involve reflection or action or both. Adolescents need to feel

71

safe enough and to be given permission to make internal journeys of exploration to and fro between their foster family and birth family as well as to travel the miles between them.

Other people, noteably social workers, foster parents and birth families may regard the issues and their outcome as clear from the outset, but the task for the adolescent is to make her own discoveries. It may not always be helpful for an initial contract to include a prematurely certain statement about where an adolescent will live at the end of a placement, so long as she can be sure that she will not be left homeless. A major task for the adolescent is to clarify, perhaps to resolve her standing in relation to her birth family or previous significant caregivers.

The possibility of the foster family acting as a secure base for exploration and risk taking moves away from the idea of fostering being set up to make rival claims for the adolescent's preoccupations, loyalty or commitment to his birth family. However, as has become apparent from most of the detailed examples considered so far, it is exceedingly difficult for foster parents to maintain a position of neutrality in the face of birth families and other caregivers who they perceive as having emotionally or physically damaged the adolescents in their care. Where neutrality proves impossible, as it seemed to have been for the Wilkinsons with Ben's family, it is best dealt with by foster parents offering a straight, open account of their view, and straight feedback on how they see the adolescent in relation to his family, with no disparagement, innuendo or anxious warnings of the birth family's power to corrupt or exploit.

Overcoming obstacles to open communication with and about an adolescent's attachment figures

Foster parents who operate a hidden agenda in relation to an adolescent's birth family or previous carers, in the hope that they can persuade the adolescent to break with them, frequently experience their worst fears being realised when the adolescent returns to a family with whom they have a destructive relationship. Where adolescents and their foster parents are unable to talk openly about the adolescent's birth family, adolescents are likely to pursue their own course regardless, but without having had the

72

benefit of a safe space for honest reflection. Hidden agenda appears to obstruct the task of reappraisal.

A more helpful approach appears to be to offer a 'mellowed' reconstruction of the evidence the adolescent presents of his family's limitations, pointing to his parents as people in their own right whose behaviour may have more to do with their own problems than with the adolescent's difficult behaviour. Timing and pacing is crucial, so that disillusionment is not anticipated, but is supported when it comes. The role of the social worker in enabling foster parents to work more openly will be discussed in Chapter 10.

Handling strong negative feelings about birth parents usually seems more of a difficulty for foster parents and residential social workers than it is for field social workers. Consequently it is particularly important for field social workers to understand that the differences may have little to do with intrinsic ability to manage strong feelings in the course of the job, and a great deal to do with the different positions of their residential and foster parent colleagues in relation to care of the adolescent. Day to day care is likely to rouse stronger feelings and it is unhelpful to feel one is being disapproved of or lectured to when these are shared.

An acknowledgement during the preparation period that feelings sometimes run high may subsequently enable field social workers and others who are not direct carers to offer a secure base to foster parents where they can feel safe enough to express what they really feel. If this is accepted as part of the job, foster parents are likely to be enabled to manage their feelings in such a way that the placement can continue to be used constructively by the adolescent.

It is equally unhelpful if either the social worker or foster parent allows an alliance to develop between them and the adolescent to the exclusion of the other party. Where this happens it is usually because they have got caught up in an adolescent's tendency to split off good and bad into different members of the team, as happened near the end of Mandy Shepperd's placement.

The course of the placements of Andy West, Mandy Shepperd and that of Tom Skipper described in Chapter 2, illustrates the way foster parents are able to keep in touch with adolescents' agenda and with their anxieties, apprehensions, fears and hopes in relation to their birth families and other caregivers. When they succeed in doing this, adolescents frequently resolve the issue wisely themselves.

Sometimes it is not so easy for either social workers or foster parents to stay with the adolescent's agenda, especially when they are concerned about the implications of the course of action the adolescent wishes to pursue, and they may need to share their position openly with the adolescent. There are also times when foster parents and social workers may catch themselves colluding in the pursuit of their own agenda to the exclusion of the adolescent, as nearly happened with Ben Little. Once they become aware of this, they can help each other back on course.

Foster parents and social workers need to operate flexibly together. When one or other becomes aware of strong negative feelings towards a birth parent or previous carer, they may need to share the difficulty explicitly, and work together on ways of handling this. Each needs to avoid getting drawn into such an exclusive alliance with the adolescent that it excludes the other. Each needs to be prepared to help the other stay in touch with the adolescent's agenda, especially if this conflicts with their own.

Collaboration between foster parents and birth parents

An adolescent's ability to reappraise his earlier attachment figures and to renegotiate his position in relation to them often appears to be influenced by his foster parents' attitude to them. Where foster parents were able to show empathy in their attitude to the adolescent's parents or other attachment figures, to collaborate with them and often to meet them, the process of reappraisal and renegotiation for the adolescent was supported. Collaboration without empathy was not helpful. There appear to be a number of possible reasons for this.

Firstly, a trusted foster parent standing alongside an adolescent while he meets with his parents may lend strength to the process of reappraisal and renegotiation. An example of this was Andy asking Mr Armstrong to talk to his foster father about his neglect. By being there with Andy and his father, Mr Armstrong was in a position to give Andy well timed feedback, confirming Andy's accurate perceptions and appraisal of his father, and himself in relation to his father.

Secondly, collaboration between foster parents and birth parents may help to confront an adolescent's delinquency or disorganised, destructive behaviour which was hitherto escaping the attention of one of both families. An example of this was when Andy's mother contacted the Armstrongs to say that she had seen Andy driving illegally in a 'borrowed' car. Such collaboration may help to extend the adolescent's experience of having a secure base as despite expressions of denial and fury they frequently seem to find it reassuring. These incidents can also help birth parents reassert a helpful balance between care and control where they have lost confidence in their ability to parent their adolescent sons and daughters.

Thirdly, collaboration involving meetings between foster parents and earlier attachment figures may help to minimise conflicts of loyalty. This may be because it reduces the likelihood of adolescents splitting between 'good' and 'bad' parents and may enable them to experience a more generalised, shared 'parental' concern for their well being.

A really difficult judgement has to be made when sabotage by birth family members reaches a level that requires the foster family to actively protect an adolescent from the unwelcome intrusion of his family. Such judgements are usually complicated by a marked degree of ambivalence between birth parents and their adolescents. At one moment the adolescent may be seeking protection and at the next seeking contact. Protection from sabotaging parents can probably only be effective when it accords with the adolescents own wishes.

Summary

Firstly in order for adolescents to experience their foster family as a secure base for exploration and risk taking, the family needs to remain consistently available, emotionally as well as physically. This involves giving their full attention to the adolescent's agenda and feelings associated with it, even though these preoccupations may seem misguided at times. Foster families need to give adolescents permission to pursue their own goals.

Secondly, honesty, open communication and straight feedback is as important in this area as any other, but more difficult. If it can be achieved, the foster family is likely to avoid the damage caused by subtle disparagement and innuendo. Sensitivity over timing and pacing is the great skill, the Armstrong's work with Andy West illustrate this beautifully.

Thirdly, collaboration between the two families may provide adolescents with a sense of containment and safety while they risk themselves in testing out the reliabiltiy of their birth family.

6 Adolescents who go missing from their foster homes: the potential for change at reunion

Episodes when adolescents go missing from their foster homes and then return frequently bewilder foster parents and often seem equally bewildering for the adolescents themselves. Foster parents in the study frequently expressed disatisfaction with their part in the interaction when the adolescent returned. Sometimes foster parents found it hard not to regard running away as a personal affront or a sign that they were failing in their care, they had assumed that once an adolescent was placed with them and offered warm, sensitive care, previous patterns of running away would cease. While this is true for many occasional runners, persistent patterns are unlikely to be broken so readily.

In practice, establishing how the pattern came to be set up in the first place may sometimes be the end point of the process, but it is not usually the most productive starting point. However, it may be helpful to explore the question of 'why now?' or what appear to be the precipitating factors, as understandings or misunderstandings about what triggered a particular incident and the meaning of this to both adolescents and foster parents can be a potent dynamic in the interaction on reunion. Where they are able to be explicit about the meaning they attach to episodes of going missing and to share this with each other on reunion, foster parents are likely to remain open and welcoming.

What happens or fails to happen between adolescent and foster parents on return from episodes of going missing provides the third focus for examining interaction across the family boundary. In common with negotiations concerned with re-entry to school or work and with testing out relationships with the adolescent's birth family, these often appear to provide a critical arena for change. Whether the change is for better or worse largely depends on how foster parents respond to the adolescent at this juncture.

Theoretically, both sociological and psychological theory point to reunion interaction following episodes of going missing as a productive focus for practioners. Milham et al (1978) writing from a perspective of social interactionist and deviancy theory found that the response made to the runner on his return to institutional care served either to amplify or reduce subsequent incidents of running. Sinclair's research on probation hostels produced a similar finding (Sinclair, 1971). Attachment theory by drawing attention to the significance of reunion behaviour of young children following unwilling separations also throws light on reunion behaviour of adolescents after 'chosen' separations. It is worth a brief diversion to review the ways in which these ideas have developed in research studies of young children and their parents.

Securely attached young children seek proximity to a parent or main caregiver following a stressful separation of a few minutes or after longer separations of a few weeks if they have been well supported by a substitute caregiver. In contrast, following longer separations of a similar length where no one person has been consistently available to the child, for example in residential care, the child's behaviour on reunion changes from proximity seeking to varying degrees of hostility and resistance, control, physical avoidance, lack of affectionate response and apparent lack of recognition of the parent. Similar patterns have been observed in the reunion response of children as young as one year in the Ainsworth Strange Situation, where an infant is introduced to a room with toys and a stranger and the parent twice leaves the room for three minutes at a time and twice returns. (Ainsworth et al., 1978) Main who has subsequently studied 6 year olds in a modified version of the Strange Situation, suggests that an insecure pattern of behaviour on reunion stems from a malignant reorganisation of feelings towards the parent which takes place over the separation and interprets this as a change in the child's internal working model in the absence of changes in the interaction. (Main, Kaplan & Cassidy, 1985)

Returning now to the adolescents in the research study, not all of them went missing from their foster homes. A wide range of criteria were used for identifying those who did, these were: repeatedly missing meals without notification to the family; coming in inconveniently later than expected without sanction, for example, two or three o'clock in the morning; staying out overnight without a mutually agreed arrangement; being absent for days or weeks (up to three or four weeks before the placement was deemed to have ended), without agreement or notification of whereabouts.

These criteria are highly dependent on the subjective experience of adolescents and foster parents; for example missing meals or coming in late might be such non-events that no-one ever thought to mention them. However it is the meaning of events to all concerned that is of interest here, as these will have a potent influence on behaviour and interaction.

On these criteria, 14 adolescents went missing. 9/14 were girls, whereas only 2/8 adolescents who did not go missing were girls. Most of these 14 adolescents went missing more than once. Apparently similar incidents sometimes brought out a different reaction in foster parents as the placement progressed. In some incidents the adolescent appeared to be displaying behaviours which accomplished more than one purpose or have more than one motivation. The four most common were:

1. Behaviour which seemed to be generally directed at avoiding current stress; whether this was stress engendered by family life, at school or work or at the prospect of an uncertain future.
2. A conflict of loyalty between foster family and members of the adolescent's birth family. This sometimes involved fears that a parent or grandparent would die in their absence or fall ill and need their care.
3. Behaviour which appeared to be activated by previous loss of parent, Sometimes this included attempts to search for a lost parent.
4. Provocative behaviour which sometimes had an element of 'hide and seek' and sometimes was infused with angry defiance.

79

Similarly, it was possible to differentiate the foster parents' responses to adolescents going missing as:

1. Avoidance of conflict or confrontation.
2. Emotional availability, empathy, welcoming back.
3. Anger, often including strong expressions of anxiety.
4. Limit setting.

In general the foster parent's ability to remain open and welcoming to the adolescent was associated with an explicit openess and sharing as to how they viewed the adolescent's behaviour and experienced its impact. When this happened, the placement was more likely to run its course and/or significant contact be maintained once it ended. Where foster parents were unable to maintain a shared, reflective stance with the adolescent, angry interaction or collusive avoidance tended to build up to a point of no return. In these cases the placement often disrupted and contact was severed.

Case Studies

Each of the following three case studies illustrates and explores a different pattern of interaction on reunion. The first case of Christine Faber was judged to have a good outcome; the other two cases of Eddie Lewis and Gina Fitzgerald did not, and illustrate in fairly extreme terms two patterns of reunion interaction which were characteristic of a number of placements. Some of the implications for social workers, working with the interaction between adolescents and caregivers around episodes of going missing, are discussed.

Christine Faber and Mrs Hatton

Going missing as a reaction to a specific event and involving some provocative behaviour. Mrs Hatton's response combines emotional availability and limit setting.

Christine, aged 16 years, was introduced in Chapter 4 when she was having difficulties getting the sort of job she wanted, she went missing following a failed job interview. Shortly before she went,

Christine and her foster mother had been discussing why she did not get the job. Christine attributed her failure to the stigma of being in care. Mrs Hatton disagreed with her, attributing it to her poor record of school attendance. Mrs Hatton takes up the story:

...I got a phone from Christine just saying, 'I'm letting you know I'm alright I'm not coming back. I've got a job and I'm not telling you where I am.' So I, just well, 'I know where you are...you're in Seaport.' She said 'I'm not!' I said 'the first time I lie to you, well you can start lying to me'. So she said ...'I've got a job. I'm working in a hotel'... I said 'that's not the way to do it Christine..O.K. if you want to go live in Seaport, I'm not saying you can and I'm not saying you can't,' I said, 'cos she has a sister lives there...She said 'Oh you won't send the police?' I said 'Well the police already know where you are because your mother's given the police your sister's address this evening'...Anyway, about threequarters of an hour later the police rang me. Said 'We've got her in the cells at Seaport, will I go for her or arrange to get her brought back?'. So...It ended that I went with the escort driver. And Christine was furious because she thought I'd...split on her, you see, although I said I wouldn't.

...Got there about 3 am and she'd smacked up one of the police women and done all sorts and she was really letting off, you know, foul mouth at them...I said 'Christine, just stop it...I'm tired and I'm hungry...just get in that car and let's get home'. And she just said, 'I'm sorry Marjorie I'm not coming...I've got a job to go to in the morning.' So she gave a load of foul mouth and that, so I just said 'get in'...O.K. she was upset. She was sick and I said to her, 'Look,...there's a way of going about things. If you want to live with your sister...we'll get your social worker over here and see what the possibilities are.'

Christine had been extremely anxious about her prospects of getting a good job, she had missed a lot of schooling while looking after her mentally ill mother. Shortly before she was due to leave school she had taken off to London with the intention of becoming a prostitute. The police speedily returned her to her home town where she was commited to care. Her only placement had been with Mrs Hatton.

By going missing, Christine had acheived her aim of finding work. She had been responsible enough to phone her foster mother. Her anger and frustration at being picked up by the police immediately after this is entirely understandable, even if misdirected at Mrs Hatton. In response, Mrs Hatton is direct and confrontational on the phone to Christine. When the police phone, Mrs Hatton is able to keep the focus of her concern on Christine and from her knowledge of her, anticipates a rapidly escalating situation which could land Christine in serious trouble. She is determined to forestall this if she can, and has to confront the full force of Christine's displaced anger face to face. She manages to respond without hostility, and stays in touch with Christine's distress.

Christine went missing again on the day of the proposed visit to Seaport designed to sanction her job and living arrangements. This time it was a week before she phoned Mrs Hatton:

> ...and just said, 'I'm alright and I'm not coming back!' Mrs Hatton said, 'Where are you?. She said, 'I'm not going to tell you because I don't want you coming for me'.

Subsequent phone calls discussed the possible consequences of returning;

> ...and then a girl rang me up. She said, 'Are you Christine's Auntie Marjorie?' I said 'Yes' and she said, 'Christine's in a lot of trouble and she needs help', so I said 'where is she?' She said 'I haven't got to tell you'. I said, well there's not a thing I can do unless you tell me where she is...Get Christine on the phone to me.' Anyway, Christine came on the phone next day and she was crying...she was really sobbing and says

> 'Marjorie, I'm in a lot of trouble, I need help' I
> said, Christine...I'll do anything within my power
> to help...but you've got to tell me where you are
> before I can help you'. She said, You'll bring the
> police and I'll get put away'. I said I won't bring
> the police and you won't get put away...you'll
> come back here'. And she just said I've got to go
> now, me money's run out'. And she really was
> sobbing and crying and we haven't heard anything
> else at all.

Mrs Hatton had to bear with the distress and anxiety that
Christine left with her for several months. After four and a half
months, when Christine was back in her home area, caring for her
mother who was terminally ill, she came over to the foster home
with her social worker for a joint retrospective interview. She
commented on her period on the run:

> I was just sort of running away from everything. I
> wasn't running for a job or owt, just running
> away...I don't know, just summat to do, I suppose.
> I just got fed up...being stuck in one place, not
> being able to find a job and just adolescence'

The discussion mulled over the second episode of going missing,
just when they had planned a visit to sanction Christine's own
arrangements: Christine's response was; 'but I wanted to do it
myself'.

It might be argued that Christine's behaviour is an entirely age-
appropriate reaction to leaving home and achieving independence;
and that only the restraints of the care order prevented her from
moving easily between her foster mother and her independent life.
Against this argument, however, is the timing of the incidents of
going missing. In each case they appeared to be a reaction to the
very process of job seeking and finding; something Christine
wanted very much to succeed in, but feared failure. There is also
Christine's own retrospective explanation which stresses she was
'running away from everything' rather than 'running to a job'.

Adolescents who go missing in reaction to a specific event
seem to leave themselves in a relatively retrievable position in

relation to their foster parents. Perhaps such absences yield explanations quite readily, enabling both adolescent and foster parents to maintain a constructive dialogue, and as in the case of Christine, to mull over the meaning together afterwards. Christine nursed her mother through her terminal illness and then, at the age of 17 years 6 months, she recontacted Mrs Hatton and asked if she might lodge with her while she was at college on a GCSE course.

Eddie Lewis and Mr and Mrs Page

Eddie Lewis, like Christine Faber, appeared to go missing in response to current stress. He may also have been reacting to his mother's death and to his grandmother's disapproval of him living with a foster family, and the conflicting advice she was giving him about what job he should seek when he left school. Although the Page's responses on his return start confrontationally, they became increasingly collusive in their avoidance of direct confrontation as the placement progressed, and the episode ends without a reunion.

Eddies mother had died when he was twelve and away at a community home with education. Before that he had been looked after by an apparently uncaring father during his mother's long illness and had run from him repeatedly. Holidays from the CH(E) were spent with his grandmother. He joined the Page family at 15 years of age, where he repeatedly missed family meals and then would turn up several hours later wanting to cook supper. They eventually put their foot down and he came in for meals. Mrs Page said:

> But what we couldn't get through to him was that there was a telephone there and if he couldn't manage to get in he could ring up...reverse the charges...It seemed as though he had a blockage there.

This raises the question of what was happening to Eddie's feelings towards his foster parents while he was absent from the foster home. Eddie ran several times in the last two months before he was due to leave school and at the same time go to school camp and then to Butlins with his foster parents. Mrs Page said:

84

he told the policeman he'd run away because he didn't like washing up...And we'd booked the holidays and everything, and even paid for the holidays...and this was when the trouble blew up. On the Friday I gave him £8 to take to school to pay for his school camp.

Eddie stayed out over the weekend and probably used the £8 to finance an outing to a football match. His foster mother checked to see if he was in school on Monday, he was, but had not paid in the £8 for the school camp:

Well the school tackled him about this £8 then, so he just didn't come home. Obviously he was too frightened...that was Tuesday...On the Friday...the social worker rang me up and he said, 'I've just met Eddie in town, he's shopping with some lads...' And I said to him, 'well, what's happening?' So he says , 'well. he says he's living there'. So I said, well, what did he say about this money that he'd stolen?'...I mean, we felt he should have said to Eddie, well, look, you've taken this £8 and you will go back and face the consequences, no matter...because I mean, he hadn't run for any other reason as far as we could see, apart from the fact that he'd stolen this money and he was frightened to come home, which was understandable.

In contrast to Mrs Hatton, these foster parents were having a great deal of difficulty finding a plausible explanation beyond the immediate one of fright. Mrs Page's connotations of the money having been 'stolen', and the school 'tackling' Eddie sound heavy handed and retaliatory and likely to precipitate panic running, yet they are followed by a striking collusive evasiveness. True, Eddie cannot face his foster parents but his social worker, it seems, cannot confront Eddie directly either, and his foster parents seem content to blame the social worker and not take any action to locate Eddie themselves and go out to him. The Page's response is in striking contrast to Mrs Hatton's overnight journey to Seaport police station. Here it seems, the foster parents could set up others to confront Eddie, but could not do it themselves, perhaps because they remained bewildered and were unable to understand or empathise with his position. Perhaps the placement ended by mutual consent. If so what were all concerned seeking to avoid? Was it their own or each others anger, or a mutual fear of rejection and desertion?

Gina Fitzgerald and Mr and Mrs Henderson

Here a provocative 15 year old engenders an increasingly angry response in her foster parents. Is this what was being avoided between Eddie Lewis and the Pages? Mrs Henderson recalls that:

> ...the first inkling of trouble I had with her, she'd been staying out...getting someone to ring me...not actually ringing herself...Sauntering in the next day as if nothing had happened...and I said 'you mustn't do it. You must ring yourself'.

Mrs Henderson's message seems mixed, Gina mustn't stay out, she must ring herself. Limit setting is unclear. These episodes of staying out increased:

> ....we really had words over this...and she said 'you give me freedom,.. and I've never had it before...and my mother went out every night', I said 'well I like to go out, Gina!' She said 'yes, but you don't go out to night clubs!' And apparently, her mother is a little bit older than me by about four years, and she said 'My mother doesn't care about the kids.' And I said 'yes, but that's me, and you know you're not...doing anything to me because you're doing it! You're saying your mother's doing it and its wrong, and you're doing the same thing!'

Either during the period when she was absent from the foster home or at the point of reunion, Gina's memories of her mother who went out at night and left her have been triggered. Her internal working model formed out of these earlier experiences is partly reversed, so that Gina appears to be acting out the behaviour she experienced from her mother who went out and left her every night; leaving Mrs Henderson to carry the fury Gina must have felt. It is as though, through her behaviour, Gina is recreating the very situation she remembers with fear from the past. Mrs Henderson appears to have difficulty hearing and responding to Gina's distressing, angry memories of her mother and separating these from the hostility she experiences as directed against herself. Mrs Henderson continues:

> ...I just really got to the end of my tether...the police came, took...again, details of my age, date of birth and who I was, and set off to look for her, brought her back at half past three in the morning...The policeman said 'we've brought you a present', and she just laughed at me and she hadn't got over the threshold and I flew at Gina and got her by her coat lapels and shook her. And I actually said, 'don't you bloody laugh at me lady, or else I'll knock you down'...it was really on impulse. I could imagine a mother hitting a child actually...I had no thought of doing that, I was going to say 'Come on in and get to bed'. And I felt a little bit sorry,...I felt shown up in front of the policeman, that I'd let myself get to that pitch with her. And we brought her into the room...And the policeman began to shout at her and say 'Look...you're a fool, you've a nice house, why are you giving this up?' And the policeman actually woke Jack up...with him shouting at her. And I didn't know, but Jack was on his way downstairs when I said to Gina, 'Up the stairs to bed', this would be four o'clock, she turned round on me...for the very first time. 'What the hell for? I'm not tired'...And luckily Jack opened the door and he said 'She's not going nowhere. I haven't had my say yet!' and he absolutely shouted and carried on at her and called her all the names

under the sun...and he said we were not being taken as mugs, if she wanted to stay she could, if she didn't she could get out.

There is a sense that the Hendersons have been drawn into the drama of the original scenario on which Gina's internal working model of self in relation to attachment figures is based. Mrs Henderson is unhappy at her lack of control, but appears unable to behave differently. Reconcilliation followed, but Gina saw herself as the victim and took no responsibility for her part in the interaction 'you're trying to send me back to a lock-up.' Both Gina and Mrs Henderson experience themselves as being punished by the other. Gina is soon off again, Mrs Henderson recalled:

> ...Two or three times in one week the police were coming...so much so that one night we reported her missing and we were very tired and we said, 'Do you have to come out ?' and they said...'of course we do, you could have her dead in bed or in the front room, or you could have her buried in the front garden'.

The police seem well and truly caught up in the pattern of provocation and murderous anger too. Eventually Gina, anticipating rejection, announced she was leaving and would not be returning. She remained firmly in control, unlike her foster mother who screamed at the emergency service when they woke her, yet again, to tell her that Gina had been found by the police: 'for goodness sake put her somewhere, put her anywhere but don't bring her here!' So they did.

Implications for practice

Where foster parents were able to come to a plausible explanation of the adolescent's behaviour as triggered by external events, they were more likely to welcome them back with warmth, empathy and perhaps some straight limit setting. If the adolescent's and foster parents' explanations were reasonable congruent, then further reflective work could continue between them, strengthening their relationship and the constructive use the adolescent could continue to make of the placement. Mrs Hatton's response to Christine going missing illustrates this well, as does the Armstrong's response to Tom Skipper, described in Chapter 2, when he returned from an unplanned stay with his newly discovered mother.

In contrast, where foster parents appeared bewildered by an adolescent's behaviour, they were far more likely to feel personally attacked or frightened by it and to have greater difficulty bearing the inevitable anxiety. In these cases there was a greater tendency for them to respond either by avoiding confrontation, sometimes in response to the adolescent's own 'avoiding' behaviour as happened with the Pages in response to Eddie Lewis, or to respond with hostility to the adolescent's apparent hostility or rejection, as happened with the Hendersons in relation to Gina Fitzgerald. Thus they were sucked into a pattern of interaction which was probably both expected and feared by the adolescent.

There appear to be a number of reasons why both foster parents and adolescents might be bewildered by the powerful dynamics operating around episodes of going missing and returning. Firstly, as discussed in Chapter 4, most adolescents in care have had repeated experiences of educational and social failure, of helplessness and worthlessness which mean that they very quickly expect that their worst fears are about to be realised. Even the prospect of a job interview, let alone failing it, precipitates panic. At such a crisis point adolescents may experience the threat of behavioural disorganisation. A foster parent who has built up an alliance with the adolescent may be able to respond helpfully by recognizing the extent of the panic, and forestall panic running, but it requires very fine tuning.

If we consider this as a form of distance regulation, then the question arises as to who will take the next step to re-establish an equilibrium. Christine was able to take the initiative through her phone calls to Mrs Hatton. In turn, Mrs Hatton's careful pacing enabled Christine, eighteen months later, to return to live with her. With more detached adolescents it may be far more difficult, we are left wishing that the Pages could have gone out to Eddie and re-established contact before the gap between them widened irretrievably. Perhaps the Armstrong's efforts to confront Tom over his socially isolated weekends, helped to hold him in some degree of proximity to them, despite his protestations.

A second reason for bewilderment is that characteristic patterns of avoidant or hostile attachment under stress for adolescents in care is triggered not only by major events like leaving school and finding a job but by everyday events such as crossing and recrossing the family boundary for ordinary purposes. Ordinary comings and goings are likely to have become associated with past experiences such as parents leaving them alone to go out every night, or their own removal into care, or parents deserting or dying while they are absent from home, or an unpredictable, rejecting response on return home. In some instances there may have been no intention to go missing, for example the early instances with Eddie and Gina, but the very fact of being away from the family may trigger obsolete internal working models so that they fear what they will find on their return and expect punishment or rejection. This may account for some of the phone calls made by adolescent's friends on their behalf, which so distressed or annoyed foster parents.

In negotiating a return, adolescents draw attention to old wounds, to the place where it hurts. In doing so they expose themselves to the possibility of further hurt by the old pattern being confirmed, or alternatively to a different, more constructive response. The likelihood that earlier distorted internal working models will be inaccessible to the adolescent (Paull, 1956; Bowlby, 1973; Main et al., 1985), suggests that the coherence and continuity of these earlier models is reinforced repeatedly as the adolescent re-enacts an earlier scenario. If this is the case, then the foster parents response on reunion is very important to challenge and disconfirm earlier models.

It is hard to over emphasise the power of the dynamic which may threaten to overwhelm both foster parent and adolescent during these incidents. It leaves all concerned feeling very shaken at the experience of so nearly or actually losing control, an experience expressed vividly by Mrs Henderson in her encounters with Gina Fitzgerald.

In the research interviews following such an incident, it was striking how often an embargo had been put on further discussion of the incident while they were together, although there were no such inhibitions on the part of foster parents after the placement had ended. While a placement was ongoing a foster parent would say 'It's all over and done with now, and I've promised we won't discuss it here.' It is as though there is an unspoken fear that to put words to such a frightening experience might actually bring about its re-enactment rather than providing a constructive opportunity for reflection by all concerned. It is possible that social workers may meet with similar reactions and feel unsanctioned in their attempts to work with the foster family including the adolescent, to try to make sense of what happened between them, what they fear they may be doing to each other, and how they might handle it differently next time.

The key is likely to lie initially in the way preparation groups for foster parents are used before the placement starts. It is helpful to have the opportunity to anticipate such experiences, through discussion of case material, role play, and ideally through discussion with other foster parents and adolescents who have been through such experiences themselves. It is also helpful to establish that some one less immediately involved such as a social worker may be able to help them in the task of reflecting on what happened and making sense of it without attributing criticism or blame.

Some foster parents, if well supported, may be able to help adolescents to use an incident of reunion interaction to examine obsolete internal working models and unlink themselves from acting out feelings belonging to one set of parents on other adult carers. The Rushmoor's work with Vicky Jones, who had been sexually abused by her father, illustrates this. They described the way Vicky ricochetted to and fro between her foster family and members of her own family:

> She tells people the most awful stories of what we do. You know, I won't let her out, I've got bars on the doors and we bully her, and her sister felt sorry for her.

By holding this perspective and the realisation that once Vicky was away from the foster home she reversed the splitting process, recreating the foster home as 'good', Vicky and the Rushmoors weathered a long and turbulent placement, and they managed to continue to welcome her back. In a joint retrospective interview Vicky's pattern of leaving and returning was the focus of their conversation:

Mrs Rushmoor	You feel you can't do it by saying 'Look, I would like to go'. You have got to have this sort of tension or scrap to prove that you have got to go, not that you want?
Interviewer	Is that right?
Vicky	What was that?
Mrs Rushmoor	You feel that you have got to create trouble here and be nasty to us to show you have got to go, not just that you want to go.
Vicky	Oh yes, definitely, that's right.

Related to this issue is the question of how best to work with adolescents who repeatedly run home or to a previous significant caregiver. Work needs to aim at minimising the conflict of loyalty. In Chapter 5 the value of collaboration between parents and foster parents was emphasised. When Christine failed to return after a weekend at home early in the placement, Mrs Hatton responded by inviting Mrs Faber to visit and providing her with some of the care that Christine was anxious that her mother was not receiving in her absence. With some relief Christine left the two of them together.

Lee Robinson invariably ran to his grandmother who was his psychological parent. His foster mother described Gran as a conspirator and worse. Lee commented on his dilemma:

> ...I'd rather go to my Grandma's..half the time and spend half the time with Reg and Ann...I'll be missing my Grandma and that even though I am seeing her every night. I'd be wondering what she is doing during the day time while I'm at work now. You see it doesn't matter what time, she could die any time, you know.

This placement ended prematurely, and when Lee was reflecting on it retrospectively, he contrasted his experience of conflicting loyalties with that of his brother who was placed in another foster family. Lee thought that his brother had experienced less conflict of loyalty, because, unlike his foster parents, his brother's foster parents had 'muddled' with his family.

Finally, it is pertinent to question how far foster families' own patterns of attachment may lead to a greater or lesser tendency to collude with the adolescent's pattern. It is possible that in the Pages we are seeing a family who operates in a distanced fashion, and in the Hendersons a family who functions in a close knit, enmeshed, ambivalent way. Foster parents may be able to become aware of their own patterns of attachment and points of vulnerability so that they may increase the range of adolescents with whom they can work effectively. This has implications for matching adolescents and foster parents which at least need to be borne in mind for the rare occasions when a choice of placement is available. These last points will be discussed in greater detail in Part 3.

7 How the end of the placement is negotiated

Adolescents will often be leaving a time limited placement at the same time that they leave care. This transition has frequently been identified as a time of stress for adolescents leaving residential and foster care (Godek, 1976; Sayer et al., 1982; Lupton, 1985; Stein and Carey, 1986).

This chapter describes and discusses characteristic patterns of behaviour which often emerge more clearly at this point than at any other time during the placement. This is because they resonate with previous experiences of unwilling separation for adolescents who are now faced with leaving foster parents, perhaps at a time not of their own choosing. For some adolescents in the sample these behaviours were hardly in evidence until the end of the placement, for others, they had been apparent throughout in ways described in previous chapters.

This chapter also considers what constitutes helpful and unhelpful responses from foster parents and social workers to adolescents negotiating the end of a placement. This is based on an understanding of the nature of adult autonomy and self reliance which was discussed in Chapter 3 where it was argued that this should not be understood to mean absolute independence from other people; throughout life, we all do better if we can be sure that we have reliable people standing behind us, available for us to turn to when we feel the need. It is not good practice to arrange for adolescents to move out to a one bedroom flat on a large housing estate, and be left to try out their 'survival' skills, with a periodic visit from their social worker, when they are lacking in the most fundamental survival skill of all; that of trusting other people to provide companionship and help and support when it is needed.

In view of this, an important criterion for evaluating the success or failure of a placement is the extent to which it has enabled a particular adolescent to draw more creatively and constructively than before on the resources of other people, whether they be family, friends, partner or professional helpers. Even where this has happened, many will become preoccupied with establishing that they will have a roof over their heads when the placement ends. In spite of provision for somewhere to live having been built into the plan worked out between the adolescent and caregiving network, they may not be able to trust that this will materialize. They may also be concerned, as they approach the end of the placement, about whether their foster parents will continue to be available and whether they will be able to continue to rely on them once the placement ends.

The end of the placement needs to be negotiated with these points in mind. This is often particularly difficult for foster parents and social workers to do, as they may be caught up with adolescents' re-enactment of earlier patterns of behaviour which functioned to protect them from further hurt in the face of unreliable relationships. They may be angry, or insistent that they can manage on their own or determined to avoid closeness. It is important not to take this at face value nor regard requests for help as childishly dependent.

At the end of the placement, adolescents are involved in leaving a family other than their birth family. The relationship between leaving the placement, leaving care and the psychosocial tasks of reappraising and renegotiating their position in relation to earlier and current attachment figures which was discussed in Chapter 5, is often a complex one.

These considerations lead on to a discussion at the end of the chapter about the circumstances in which it is likely to be appropriate or inappropriate to use time limited family placements for adolescents in care.

Patterns of behaviour and interaction over the ending of the placement

In the study, a starting point was made for developing a framework for considering patterns of behaviour and interaction over the ending of the placement, by identifying three sequential time periods. The first, which could in some cases extend from the start of the placement, covered the period anticipating and preparing for its ending. The second covered a period of approximately six weeks over the ending. The third covered what happens between adolescent and foster family after the end of the placement, at least for a long enough period to establish whether the relationship between them continued or not.

It was possible in the study to make judgements at each stage about the feelings expressed by the adolescent about the ending of the placement, their level of functioning at school or work and in their leisure activities, and the nature and quality of the interaction between adolescent and foster parents. This framework is set out in Table 7.1.

Depending on an adolescent's behaviour as they anticipate the end of the placement it may be possible to make at least a tentative prediction of the likely shape of subsequent stages, and to plan appropriate intervention. In the study, most of the adolescents could be grouped according to these three broad patterns of behaviour:

Group 1. Adolescents who are able to stay in touch with a range of feelings relating to the end of the placement, including anxiety, sadness, pleasurable anticipation and challenge. They can plan ahead, go on functioning reasonably well and involve their foster parents constructively at all stages. Less positively, they tend to display a rather brittle self reliance, managing the move by taking control and sometimes moving out precipitately ahead of time. They may lack confidence that they will be welcomed back to the foster home once they have left.

Group 2. Adolescents who demonstrate very limited affect before, during and after the placement ends. Their behaviour deteriorates, and they do not draw on their foster parents' help. They are

Table 7.1: A framework for considering patterns of behaviour and interaction around the end of the placement

		Group 1	Group 2	Group 3
Feelings expressed	Preparation for ending	In touch with a range of feelings (of anxiety and sadness, anger) related to ending	Very limited affect when anticipating ending	Dominated by anger – often with marked angry mood swings
	Over ending	In touch with a range of feelings relating to ending	Limited affect over ending of placement	Dominated by anger, focused on foster parents
	After ending	In touch with a range of feelings about ending and about the foster family	Limited affect in relation to foster family	Relationship with foster parents continues to be characterised by angry mood swings
Social functioning	Preparation for ending	Able to plan ahead. Able to go on functioning at same level at school or work and socially	Unable to plan. Deterioration in functioning at school or work and socially	Anticipates rejection. Deterioration in functioning at school or work and socially
	Over ending	Stays with plans, and goes on functioning at work and in social life	Deterioration or breakdown in functioning at work or socially	Deterioration or breakdown in functioning which may include aggressive delinquent acting out
	After ending	Continues to function at roughly same level as before at work and in social life	Continued deterioration or breakdown in functioning at work or socially	Deterioration or breakdown in functioning continues linked with further outbursts of aggression
Interaction between adolescent and foster parents	Preparation for ending	Draws on foster parents' help	Doesn't involve foster parents in plans	Stormy, angry interaction, often with escalating rows
	Over ending	Uses foster parents' help over move out	Doesn't involve foster parents in plans	High level of angry conflict, sometimes interspersed with reconciliations
	After ending	Continued contact which is used constructively	No constructive contact	Contact continues to swing in and out of angry outbursts and rows

passive and unself-reliant and give the impression that if they were allowed to, they would stay for ever. Their foster parents tend to feel they are doing all the worrying for them.

Group 3. Adolescents whose behaviour and relationships are dominated by anger around the end of the placement. Often this results in escalating rows, sometimes with rapid swings from hostile attack to reconcilliation. Their foster parents often feel murderously angry at them and have difficulty controlling their fury. They may make constructive use of their foster parents once the placement has ended.

Clearly, these are similar patterns to those described and discussed in Chapter 6 when adolescents were reunited with their foster parents following episodes of going missing. As well as these three main patterns of behaviour, some adolescents showed behaviour that was intermediate between Groups 1 and 2. They were able to anticipate the end of the placement, but viewed it with a reluctance verging on trepidation. Like those in Group 2 they would like to stay for longer and it would probably help them if they could. They were more adept than those in Group 2 at building their ex-foster parents into their future support network. Tom Skipper, described in Chapter 2 is an example of an adolescent in this intermediate group. In addition, some adolescents showed more mixed patterns of behaviour and interaction, these are considered individually later in the chapter.

The characteristics of the subgroups

In Table 7.2 patterns of behaviour shown by adolescents around the end of the placements is charted. The numbers correspond to the three broad positions or patterns of behaviour summarised in Table 7.1. The final column on the right shows the predominant position of each adolescent. Four adolescents showed behaviour characteristic of Group 1. The behaviour of three adolescents was intermediate between Groups 1 and 2. Seven adolescents (all males) showed behaviour characteristic of Group 2. Four adolescents (all females) showed behaviour characteristic of Group 3. Four adolescents showed a mixed pattern of behaviour.

Table 7.2: Patterns of behaviour shown by adolescents around the end of the placement

	A PREPARATION AND LEAD-UP			B OVER ENDING			C AFTER ENDING			Predominant position of adolescent
	Feelings	Funct-ioning	Foster Parents	Feelings	Funct-ioning	Foster Parents	Feelings	Funct-ioning	Foster Parents	
PROSPECTIVE SAMPLE										
Clare Dobson	(3)	(3)	(3)	(3)	(3)	(3)	not known	not known	(2)	(3)
Paul Elliott (i)	(2)	(2)	(2)	(2)	(2)	(2)	(2)	(2)	(2)	(2)
Christine Faber	(2)	(1)	(2)	(1)	(1)	(1)	(1)	(1)	(1)	(1)
Kevin Flynn	(3)	(2)	(2)	not known	(3)	(2)	not known	not known	(2)	mixed
Ben Little	(2)	(1/2)	(2)	(2)	(2)	(2)	(1/2)	(2)	(2)	(2)
Julie Piggott	(2/1)	(1)	(1)	(3)	(3)	(3)	(1)	(2)	(2)	mixed
Mandy Shepperd	(1)	(1/2)	(2)	(2)	(2)	(2)	(3)	(1)	(2)	mixed
Tom Skipper	(2)	(1/2)	(1)	(2)	(2/3)	(2)	(1/2)	(1/2)	(1/2)	(1/2)
Andy West	(1)	(1)	(1)	(2)	(1)	(1)	not known	(1)	(2)	(1)
Diane White	(1)	(1)	(1)	(2)	(1)	(2)	(1)	(1)	(1)	(1)
Veronica Williams	(2)	(1)	(1)	(2)	(2)	(2)	(1)	(1/2)	(2)	mixed

99

Table 7.2 (Continued)

	A PREPARATION AND LEAD-UP			B OVER ENDING			C AFTER ENDING			Predominant position of adolescent
	Feelings	Funct-ioning	Foster Parents	Feelings	Funct-ioning	Foster Parents	Feelings	Funct-ioning	Foster Parents	
RETROSPECTIVE SAMPLE										
Wendy Bell	(1)	(1)	(1)	(1)	(1)	(1)	(1)	(1)	(1)	(1)
Wayne Brett	(2)	(2)	(2)	(2)	(2)	(2)	not known	not known	(2)	(2)
Paul Elliott (ii)	(2)	(1)	(2)	(2)	(2)	(2)	not known	not known	(2)	(2)
Gina Fitzgerald	(3)	(3)	(3)	(3)	(3)	(3)	(3)	(3)	(3)	(3)
Dawn Gibson	(3)	(3)	(3)	(3)	(3)	(3)	(1)	(3)	(1)	(3)
Vicky Jones	(3)	(3)	(3)	(3)	(3)	(3)	(3)	(3)	(3)	(3)
Tim Larkin	(1)	(1)	(1)	(1)	(2)	(1)	(1)	(2)	(1)	(1/2)
Eddie Lewis	(2)	(2)	(2)	(2)	(2)	(2)	not known	not known	(2)	(2)
Frank Little	(2)	(2)	(2)	(2)	(2)	(2)	not known	(2)	(2)	(2)
Rose Phillips	(2)	(2/3)	(1)	(2)	(2/3)	(2)	(1)	(2)	(1)	(1/2)
Lee Robinson	(2)	(2)	(2)	(2)	(2)	(2)	(1)	(2)	(1/2)	(2)
Mark Robinson	(2)	(2)	(2)	(2)	(2)	(2)	(1/2)	(2)	(1/2)	(2)

Case Studies

Group 1. Diane White

Diane's placement started when she was 16 years of age, it had been planned to run for six months to one year as an intermediate step between a community home with education and independent living. She had tested out her foster parents reliability during the placement through the support they gave her when starting work and during a major crisis when she was remanded back at her community home on drugs charges after she renewed a past relationship with a drug addicted boyfriend. Her foster parents subsequently supported her through her boyfriend's death from a drug overdose. Diane had also worked hard exploring the reliability and limitations of her birth family as a future base, and with the exception of one sister, found them wanting.

In preparing for the end of the placement, Diane did some practical planning, getting things together that she would need in a bedsitter, helped and advised by her foster parents. There was an argument between them about the timing of the move, Diane was impatient to be off but the Hendersons felt she was rushing. The bedsitter was found by her social worker who also planned to help her with the move. At the point of the move it seemed difficult for Diane and her social worker to allow the Hendersons to help as well. Staying in the same job over this period provided Diane with a sense of continuity through a network of workmates but when her job ended a few weeks after she had moved out, depression and loneliness caught up with her. At that point she regretted having made such a precipitate move.

The Hendersons had left Diane with many verbal invitations to visit them but she was unable to take the initiative to contact them. Their first meeting after the end of the placement was at the research interview which was arranged to take place in Diane's bedsitter, six weeks after Diane had left the foster home. The Hendersons recognised Diane's depression and vulnerability and invited her back to stay for a few days there and then. The Hendersons commented that they had never seen anyone pack a bag so fast! After that, staying in touch was a bit easier, but Diane was still left to take the initiative. Gradually the relationship between them was re-established, and it appeared to have been renegotiated on a more adult-to-adult basis and lasted for several years.

Implications for the social worker's task. Despite disagreeing with Diane about the timing of the move out, the Hendersons managed, through compromise, to prevent a rift developing between them. It would probably have helped them all if the Hendersons and Diane's social worker could have shared the job of helping Diane on moving day, this would have enabled Diane to have shown them all her bedsitter and the prospect of continued contact with the Hendersons could have been built in more firmly from the start. The Hendersons might have been encouraged to plan a get-together with Diane soon after the move. What subsequently became clear was that the Hendersons were finding it as difficult as Diane to initiate contact, yet both they and Diane wanted it. While Diane's social worker necessarily concentrated on helping Diane survive in her bedsitter, there was some equally important work for her to do, focussed on the relationship between Diane and the Hendersons, affirming to Diane, the Henderson's continued concern for her and to the Hendersons, Diane's continued wish to see and visit them.

Group1/2. Tim Larkin

Tim was nearly 18 years when his placement with the Armstrongs started. He had been committed to care at 11 years and following severe depression and self-mutilation was admitted to psychiatric hospital when he was 13 years and remained there until he was 17 years old. At this point Tim persuaded his new social worker to let him try a one year family placement. He had no idea how to relate to his peers and the young adult children of the family protected him in the pub when he made near disastrous mistakes, following this up with vigorous feedback afterwards about the likely consequences of his behaviour. His foster parents main worry was that a year would prove too short for Tim to make up so much lost ground. Tim anticipated the end reluctantly and made sure he left the door open for his return:

| *Tim* | I don't want to leave unless I'm kicked out...No, I mean, I'd leave after my time is up. Like in |

prison, your time is up; that's a joke. When July comes and I'm eighteen, if I've got somewhere to go, I'll go. But if it doesn't work I'll contact Liz [Mrs Armstrong] again and see if I can come back.

Mrs Armstrong Well, you know, that's what we thought.

Not only were the practicalities of life in lodgings and managing to get up for work discussed openly, but also Tim's depression.

Mr Armstrong There's going to be a time very shortly when he's going to run out of jobs to go to, and it would be O.K. all the time you were here, being out of work. But I'm a bit worried about when you leave here because, by and large, you haven't been badly depressed since you've been here, you've had your moments when you've felt pretty rough...

Tim Well, I think you get more depressed if you are on your own than you do if you are in company.

Tim found a landlady not far from his foster home, hoping she would provide company. The landlady had similar hopes and poured out her disappointments and troubles to Tim until he was walking the streets at night to avoid her. Fortunately he could return to his foster home where the Armstrongs suggested he might do better in a flat. Tim, however was clear about his own proposed solution:

Tim I need somebody round me. That's one of the reasons I want to get married so soon, you see, because I need somebody round me all the time.

When Tim next moved out it was to the home of his girlfriend's parents. Tim and his girlfriend married and for the next three years they lived, with their two young children, closely bounded by two sets of 'grandparents', that is his wife's parents and his ex-foster parents. There was frequent contact between the grandmothers.

103

Implications for the social worker's task. Tim, like Tom Skipper, was not able to maintain the level of functioning at work that he had achieved in the foster home and was mainly out of work. A social worker in this situation may be able to explore ways and means for the placement to be extended, otherwise they may anticipate the need to offer a lot of intensive help to the adolescent when it ends.

Group 2. Ben Little

Aspects of Ben's placement with the Wilkinsons were described in Chapter 5, in relation to Ben's efforts to test out the possibility of eventually setting up of a home with his older brothers.

When it came to practical planning, Ben was unable to think ahead, or even envisage in any real way that the placement would end at eighteen. About five months before Ben's eighteenth birthday, his foster parents were voicing their anxieties; it seemed to them that they were left with all the planning and all the worry, and that all their attempts to teach Ben simple survival skills like budgetting and basic cooking had failed. Near the end of the placement, however, Ben did take some tentative steps to find a small hostel where he and his brothers might live. For the first time in the placement Ben started to disagree openly with his foster parents and social worker about what might be considered suitable accommodation for him as they appeared to be firmly of the opinion that Ben would do better in lodgings on his own rather than sharing accommodation with his brothers.

Ben got his way and moved to the hostel. Immediately after the move Ben's personal appearance and hygiene deteriorated and he lost his job. With the help of the hostel staff who set firm limits, his deterioration was stemmed and he regained his equilibrium. He maintained only minimal contact with his foster home but spoke with positive feeling of his time there and of how he missed them. In contrast to Diane White, no fortuitous or planned intervention enabled them to get back in contact with one another.

Implications for the social worker's task. When the placement seems likely to end with adolescent and foster parents in major disagreement, the most helpful role for a social worker is to try to hold the tension between them, allowing for the possibility that there may be some valid arguments on both sides. This point will be further developed later in the chapter, in relation to Julie Piggott and in Chapter 10. At the end of his placement, Ben proved not to be as totally passive as the Wilkinsons had come to experience him. Perhaps a social worker from a vantage point outside this powerful dynamic between adolescent and foster parents, might be able to hear and take seriously Ben's wish to move to a hostel with his brothers. This would involve drawing attention to the difficulties Ben and the Wilkinsons were having in working together, and to the difficulty the Wilkinsons were having in staying in touch with and respecting Ben's agenda where it differed from their own.

Group 3. Dawn Gibson

Dawn's entry to school was described in Chapter 4. Dawn had been in care since she was 12 years of age, frequently stealing and absconding such that she was never in one place for long, apart from one particular assessment centre to which she returned with relief, periodically. Dawn was placed with Mrs Hatton when she was 15 years of age. From the start, the theme of interaction between herself and her foster mother was mainly one of nagging and being nagged. This developed into a related theme, that of the pursued and the pursuer as she followed the local fairs from place to place, staying out to sleep with her boyfriend in his caravan. The placement lasted seven months, much of it focussing directly or indirectly on the likelihood of it ending. Dawn prepared for rejection after about three months in the placement:

Dawn	She seemed not to want me, after a while, with getting into trouble.
Interviewer	How did she show you that?
Dawn	She stopped nagging at me and she said she wasn't bothered what I did, and stopped nagging me. So when she didn't nag me, I'm off and I knew then that she didn't care much.

Mrs Hatton, independently, gave a very similar version. Dawn's behaviour shifted from stealing food from the house to feed the lads at the fair, to shoplifting, burglary and then stealing from other girls in the foster home. Then it entered another phase:

Mrs Hatton   Dawn was absolutely certain I was doing all I could to get her sentenced...and this I think was when she did change, she was nasty. I think she started pilfering a lot more then...taking my bedroom stuff...which showed she was getting back at me.

Dawn was remanded in custody, awaiting charges of burglary and shoplifting but the Court allowed her to return to the foster home on a deferred sentence. Mrs Hatton soon found shoplifted clothes in the house, and when she called the police they both knew there would be no question of Dawn returning this time.

When Dawn reviewed the placement soon after it had ended, from the safety of her familiar assessment centre, she considered it had been a disaster. Mrs Hatton felt angry that she had been left to call the police and guilty about doing so, when she had promised Dawn she would never reject her. Getting back in contact with each other was shaky at first but gained momentum. Dawn spent days and a weekend back at the foster home for her birthday and Christmas, which they both enjoyed. They agreed that things were much better between them than they ever had been during the placement.

The idea that anger, as a form of attachment behaviour, has the potential function of coercing an attachment figure into proximity, is potentially helpful for making sense of what is going on here. Dawn was reassured when Mrs Hatton pursued her round the fairs and despaired when she stopped doing this. Bowlby (1973) further recognises dysfunctional anger, when a person becomes so intensely angry with his attachment figure that the bond between them is weakened rather than strengthened:

Anger with a partner becomes dysfunctional also whenever aggressive thoughts or acts cross the narrow boundary between being deterrent and being revengeful. It is at this point, too, that feeling ceases to be the 'hot displeasure' of anger, and may become, instead, the malice of hatred.(Bowlby, 1973, p. 249).

Implications for the social worker's task. When Mrs Hatton called the police for the last time, both Dawn and Mrs Hatton feared that this would be experienced by Dawn as being 'abandoned' yet again. In fact, by ending the placement before anger became any more dysfunctional, the foster home appears to have been preserved as a secure base for future return. Mrs Hatton hints that she would have appreciated a social worker stepping in to share the work and responsibility of ending the placement, so that she was not left to take all the difficult decisions on her own.

Adolescents showing mixed patterns of behaviour at the end of the placement

Four adolescents in the study who showed a mixed pattern of relating and functioning during the placement, reacted in more extreme ways than might have been anticipated over the ending and in each case they and their foster parents lost contact with each other after the placement ended. I shall first consider Veronica Williams and Mandy Shepperd who behaved in very detached ways, apparently losing touch with their feelings over the move.

Veronica Williams. Veronica and her birth parents had a mutually destructive pattern of interaction, associated with Veronica making several suicide attempts. Much effort by her social worker and foster parents was put into acting as a buffer between Veronica's provocative pleas to her family for reinstatement and their responding threats of harsh punishment or murder. At intervals members of the family would invade the foster home, ostensibly to carry out their threats, and Veronica would ask to be hidden from them. She appeared well settled with the Knights and was discussing plans for moving into a flat sometime in the future. The end came suddenly and unexpectedly after nineteen months, it was described by Mrs Knight:

> She got a telephone call from her brother....and the brother said he'd some good news for her and you know what Veronica's like, 'Oh, what is it?'...He said, 'We've decided that we love you'. And she said ,'Oh'...I heard this conversation and you couldn't have believed it if you hadn't heard it yourself. And he said, 'Your mother's decided that you can come home now because she's

forgiven you and she loves you now'. And she said 'Does she really love me?' And I heard this 'Does she really love me?' you see, so I opened the door and I said, 'Who is it, Veronica?'. She said 'It's my brother, he's got some good news for me; my mother loves me'. So I said, 'Oh, I wonder what's brought that on'. The conversation went on from one thing to another and obviously the mother had told the son to ring up and say she could go home now...

Veronica left at once, she subsequently regretted her decision but seemed unable to take any responsibility for it, 'they [her family] made her do it'. Nor could she renew contact with her foster parents. It is not easy to see what more could have been done to prevent this happening. All attempts to work with Veronica's family had failed. Veronica had been working regularly with her social worker to reappraise her feelings about her family, which were similar to those described by Sinason (1990) as 'passionate, lethal attachments':

> Because deprivation can lead to longing for further physical contact, brutality can be mistaken for passion, as can mad possessiveness...We have also to understand that it is attachment, the most basic of human needs, we are dealing with, not a 'stupid' perverted choice of the child's. (Sinason, 1990, p.76).

Implications for the social worker's task. Veronica clearly needed longer for this painful work of reappraisal; the protection afforded by commital to care might have provided the extra time and space she needed.

Mandy Shepperd. Mandy Shepperd's efforts to reappraise and test out a series of previous caregivers was discussed in Chapter 5. Having carefully planned to move with a girlfriend to a semi-independent living unit, she persuaded her friend not to go on holiday, 'because they needed the money for equipment'. Mandy then departed for a continental holiday herself, with her previous foster parents the Martins, leaving the painful emotional transition and all the physical work of the move to her friend. After the move she was well supported by friends and maintained a good level of functioning at college, but her contact with Mrs Hatton was minimal and continued to be hostile.

It is possible that both Veronica and Mandy had experienced consistently incompatible messages from parent figures, for example, parental behaviour may be rejecting while parents insist they love a child. As adolescents they are faced with a grave dilemma; are they to accept the picture as they experienced it or as their caregiver insists is true? Bowlby (1988) in a paper entitled 'On knowing what you are not supposed to know and feeling what you are not supposed to feel' enlarges on this phenomenon. On this view, Veronica just managed to maintain an alternative version of reality of her rejecting parents during the placement but when invited home swung into complete compliance with her parents' view. The two worlds had to be kept apart, as they had been during the placement, to avoid cognitive breakdown. Mandy's cut-off from Mrs Hatton and her girl friend may have avoided the work of mourning the end of the placement, so that she was left with a separate, encapsulated experience of two years in her foster home which had to be kept apart from her subsequent experience.

Implications for the social worker's task. Where a social worker suspects that earlier events and experiences have left an adolescent with incompatable messages about herself in relation to attachment figures, the task is in helping her discover what these events probably were and what her conflicting feelings are now for the people concerned.

Kevin Flynn. Kevin behaved over the end of the placement in ways which were sometimes implicitly and sometimes openly hostile, having presented more mixed patterns of functioning previously. Kevin's foster parents seemed only able to operate by heavily controlling his every move. Mrs Goldman opened a savings account with Kevin's money in her name and then reminded him of an earlier incident where he had stolen from her and had not repaid the money. Kevin always had to accompany the Goldmans on outings as they did not trust him in the house on his own. Inevitably, such a state of affairs was unsustainable, the first time Kevin was left in the house on his own, he broke into the gas meter and went missing with the money.

Implications for the social worker's task. The likelihood that when foster parents operate on a hidden agenda the very scene they fear will be acted out was discussed in Chapter 5 and is well illustrated here. This could probably have been foreseen, although in this particular case the implication appeared to be that the Goldmans were unlikely to be effective foster parents for any adolescents. Practice in such situations is discussed in Chapter 10.

Julie Piggott. Julie Piggott's approach to the end of the placement had been a mixture of brittle self-reliance and passive dependency until a new social worker took over. She considered that Julie at 17 years should not be constrained within a foster family but had a right to be free to lead an independent life. A hostile alignment of Julie and her social worker against Mrs Hatton escalated rapidly, leaving Mrs Hatton angry, hurt and impotent. Once in a flat Julie bitterly regretted the precipitate move and talked of wishing she had been adopted by her foster mother, but neither she nor Mrs Hatton were able to take the initiative in re-establishing contact.

Implications for the social worker's task. This is an example of the social worker who was responsible for the adolescent identifying closely with her. In such a situation a second social worker, responsible for promoting effective working within the caregiving network, would be needed to enable the adolescent's social worker and foster parent to work constructively together, despite their disagreement. This issue is discussed in the following section and in chapter 10.

General implications for practice

While brief comments have been offered in the previous section on the role of the social worker in particular cases, this final section discusses some general issues relating to the end of the placement and explores their implications for practice. These include how to prevent irrevocable splits developing between adolescent and foster parents, how the way in which the ending of the placement is managed might help or hinder the adolescent reappraise and renegotiate their position with their birth parents and other significant earlier attachment figures, how the foster family might continue to be experienced by the adolescent as a secure base to which they might refer or return from time to time, and what are the advantages and disadvantages of time limited placements and for whom?

How to prevent an irrevocable split developing between
adolescent and foster parents around the end of the placement

This has already been discussed in Chapter 5 in relation to the importance of foster parents or social workers avoiding the sort of alliance with the adolescent which excludes their birth parents. One aspect of this involves ways in which foster parents and social workers work together to hold the tension between presenting the adolescent with what seems a sensible adult solution, about where she will live and when she will move out, and actively helping the adolescent in her apparently less sensible solutions, usually relating to where she is going to live and with whom.

As long as all concerned are able to envisage the possibility of alternative solutions, each with some positive aspects, the doors are likely to remain open. What can all too easily happen is for an involuntary split to occur at this stage between social worker and foster parents, one pursuing the 'adolescent' solution and the other pursuing the 'adult' solution, both with great conviction. With Ben, his social worker formed an exclusive alliance with his foster parents. With Julie, her social worker formed an alliance with her which excluded her foster mother. If Julie Piggott is left feeling she has been helped into her flat by her social worker against the wishes of her foster mother, it may be much more difficult for her to recontact her foster parents when things aren't going too well later, and when her social worker is unable to sustain the level of support that was implied during the period around the move.

In Chapter 10 the concept of containment is discussed and the possibility of foster parents collaborating with other professionals and the adolescent's birth family to create a 'coffer dam' for an ambivalent adolescent.

*Ways in which the management of the end of the placement
might help or hinder adolescents reappraise and renegotiate
their position in relation to birth parents and other significant
earlier attachment figures*

One hope running through time limited placements is that by the
end adolescents who have experienced severe failures of parental
care in the past and who may themselves be trying to make sense
of having in some, often indefineable, way failed their parents,
will have reached a more realistic appraisal of their significant
attachment figures and themselves in relation to them.

Internal pressures, such as those seen in an extreme form in
Veronica William's destructive attachment to her parents which
had developed out of years of severe emotional abuse may obstruct
this process and be extremely difficult to alleviate. However,
some of the obstructions to the process of reappraisal continuing
over the ending of the placement are external ones. In many cases,
adolescents' precipitate return to an unchanged, unsatisfactory
home appears to have more to do with the care system than with
the adolescent or their foster parents. The more subtle processes of
renegotiation that go on for most adolescents who remain in their
own homes appear to be overridden for adolescents in care who
get very anxious and preoccupied about establishing that they will
have a roof over their heads when the placement ends and they
leave care. Even though provision for somewhere to live may
have been built into a plan worked out between them and their
social worker they may not be able to trust that this will happen.

If renegotiation becomes linked with strong attachment
behaviour, this can override any attempts at realistic reappraisal.
The danger is that adolescents return home unchanged themselves
and history repeats itself. Although Andy had reappraised his
father to the point of disillusionment, if not forgiveness, it was
quite possible that his rather frantic move out of care to his mother
was more to do with attachment behaviour than exploration.

Pressures may also arise from anxieties within the network of
helping professionals about how the adolescent will fare in the
adult world. Examples have been cited in the previous section of
exclusive alliances developing around the end of a placement that
either fail to contain the adolescent or the foster parents. Another
example, given in Chapter 6, was of Lee Robinson, where

professional alliances appeared to exclude Lee's birth family, leading to such a conflict of loyalty for Lee that the placement disrupted.

Alliances that exclude members of the caregiving network are likely to raise an adolescent's level of anxiety, thus triggering strong attachment behaviour. This is only likely to be assuaged when the adolescent again experiences being emotionally contained by effective collaboration within the caregiving network.

The foster home as a continuing secure base for the adolescent

In order to experience their ex-foster home as a secure base to which they may return when they feel the need, adolescents need the experience of leaving and being welcomed back; an idea which was explored in Chapter 6 in relation to adolescents going missing and returning. In a similar way, trial separations, such as Tim Larkin experienced during his first move out from the Armstrongs and Diane White experienced during her period on remand in custody, may go some way to reassuring adolescents that there is a home to return to.

This links with a concept from family systems theory, that of the permeability of the boundary between the family and the world outside. Foster parents such as the Hendersons, who go to court and stand by an adolescent who has been remanded in custody, and state they are willing to have her back, demonstrate they are prepared to move outside the four walls of the house and draw her back with them. I am suggesting here that this needs not only to be demonstrated repeatedly during placements but also after placements end. A family with rather impermeable boundaries is unlikely to do this or see the need for it. The things the family are prepared to do with the adolescent outside the foster home and eventually the contact they maintain when the adolescent eventually has their own home base are often of great significance to him or her.

For this to happen, foster parents need to be assured of their value to the adolescent. Tim Larkin made this clear to his foster parents before he left, and Dawn Gibson made it abundantly clear as soon as she had left. Foster parents are given fewer assurances by adolescents like Ben Little or Diane White. With a passive, detached adolescent like Ben, foster parents tend to feel they have made no impact and do not matter to him. The disparagement of the detached and the hostility of the angry adolescent can be powerfully undermining to foster parents. Where a placement ends rapidly in an unplanned way foster parents are often left feeling guilty and depressed, with a sense of having failed. Understood this way, it is not surprising that they are reluctant to 'intrude' and fail to recognise how difficult it may be for the adolescent to take the initiative. Social workers have a vital role to play in 'constructive reformulation' of the fostering relationship, in order to reassure foster parents that they are valued by the adolescent, when they are having difficulty holding onto the evidence for this. This is discussed further in chapter 10.

What are the advantages and disadvantages of time limits on placements, and for whom?

Foster parents are likely to see advantages in time limits for adolescents like Ben, who are behaving in a passively detached way. Time limits provide a foreseeable end to what might otherwise seem an intolerable burden. Ben's foster parents were able to keep going longer by knowing there was an agreed end. There may be similar advantages for some adolescents whose capacity for attachment is greater than Ben's, but who still need to find ways of distancing themselves from the discomfort of close emotional relationships, Diane White and Dawn Gibson, for example. In these cases it is unlikely the adolescent would have agreed to embark on such an emotionally demanding venture as family placement if it had seemed from the outset to have no end. For adolescents like Tim Larkin and perhaps Tom Skipper whose capacity for attachment enabled them to make up some lost ground, time limits appear to have more disadvantages than advantages unless they can be used very flexibly, with repeated reviews and extensions.

We have to acknowledge that for older adolescents in care, all placements are in some sense 'time limited'. The main distinction seems to be between setting an end point from the start, when the adolescent will move out, regardless of their readiness to move, and those where they can be assured that there foster home is there for as long as they need it. Provided both adolescent and foster family can tolerate this arrangement, and ways can be found to support it administratively and statutorily, it would appear to be in the best interests of most adolescents in care.

Social workers need to hold the balance between acknowledging the constraints and recognising the value of work that can be achieved within time limits and not hiding behind bureaucratic inevitabilities. The time dimension of the eighteenth birthday does not have to be the only consideration; it is possible for there to be careful, creative planning concerning the continuing relationship between adolescent and foster parents beyond this date, even when it is not possible for the placement to continue. In the future this should be supported by the Children Act, 1989, which makes provision for aftercare up to 21 years of age.

As in other aspects of social workers and foster parents work together, flexibility of roles is important around the end of the placement. Both may need to be fully involved with the adolescent over aspects of the move if the message is to be one of continuing concern and availability. Each can contribute to being alert to what is happening for the adolescent, and between themselves and the adolescent, and together they are more likely to be able to stem the worst consequences of the end of the placement.

Part 3
PROVIDING A SECURE BASE FOR THE ADOLESCENT

8 Understanding the tasks of the placement in the light of attachment theory

Part 2 provided some detailed accounts of the experiences of adolescents and foster parents and the negotiations between them as the adolescent moves to and fro across the family boundary. The issues raised are likely to preoccupy many adolescents but particularly adolescents in care.

In Part 1 it was suggested that the transition to adult life involves a series of psychosocial tasks, each contributing to a developing sense of self through reorientation to a range of key relationships. Adolescents in care who have not previously had the experience of a secure base from which to negotiate this transition are likely to find themselves in difficulties; they may find it difficult to trust adults or peers and may play an active part in perpetuating unhelpful ways of relating to them. When this is the case, placement in foster care may enable them to make more constructive relationships. In Part 2 ways in which this change might come about or might be hindered, were illustrated.

Part 3 draws together the theoretical and practical themes that ran through our discussion of these experiences; it considers the nature of the change that may take place, ways in which change might be understood and assessed and ways in which foster parents, social workers and other members of the caregiving network might help the adolescent to successfully negotiate the transition to adult life.

Chapter 8 considers how to understand and assess adolescents

119

in the light of their potential for changing the way they relate to significant people in their lives. In this chapter, in line with the approach in Part 2, the foster parent is regarded as the person who will be doing much of the direct work with the adolescent and the focus is on the dyadic relationship between foster parent and adolescent, with the foster parent working in such a way as to offer the adolescent a secure base for negotiating the transition to adult life. The social worker's role is described in terms of working with the adolescent and foster parents to assess the adolescent and understand the interaction.

Chapter 9 focusses on assessing and understanding the foster family as a system. Ways in which the foster family as a whole might operate to provide a secure base for the adolescent are considered. The potential for change and some difficulties which may arise when adolescents and foster families who have different styles of relating find themselves under the same roof, are also discussed. In this chapter the social worker's role is considered mainly in terms of assessment of the foster family and understanding of the interaction between adolescent and foster family.

In Chapter 10 consideration is given to some common difficulties between members and subsystems of the wider caregiving network which includes the adolescent and foster family members. Here a new role for the social worker is described; that of constructing a secure base for the caregiving network which will enable its members to work together with the adolescent in his or her best interests.

Principles for understanding and working with adolescents and their foster parents

Arising out of the detailed examination of the interaction between adolescents and foster parents, in the light of attachment theory, a number of principles can be deduced. These principles may be applied to understanding the adolescents, and to the interaction between them and their foster parents.

1. As a result of their previous experiences, many adolescents who are looked after by the local authority have considerable difficulties in using other peoples' help; either they are only

able to fend for themselves or they repeatedly subvert their own efforts to cope and to make satisfying relationships. Their difficulties in making alliances with helpful adults and peers are likely to put them at a disadvantage when they are trying to make their way in the world as young adults. The remedy, therefore, has to be more complicated than merely offering adolescents opportunities to learn practical 'survival skills' before they leave care, although these are necessary too.

2. In an optimum position adolescents and adults are able to feel comfortable in a wide range of interactions within a significant relationship, they are able to enjoy intimacy and also to operate independently at some distance from their family or friends, and they are able to move easily between these positions. In contrast, many adolescents looked after by the local authority lack this flexibility. They may either cling anxiously or keep the people who are important to them at arms length, they may have difficulties in trusting other people or committing themselves to close relationships with adults or peers.

3. These inflexible patterns of behaviour have a tendency to be self perpetuating, as the adolescents concerned are likely to be active partners in keeping things the same. Change may come about simply through experiencing a different quality of relationship with foster parents, but is more likely to involve adolescents reflecting on what has happened to them in earlier relationships and exploring the perceptions and feelings that close relationships engender in them.

4. Events involving interaction between adolescents and foster parents on the boundary between the family and the world outside the family may be regarded as potential junction points where change in an adolescent's developmental pathway may occur for better or worse.

5. While adolescents may begin to trust their foster parents and to gain confidence in negotiating the transition to adult life, during the placement, once the placement ends they may not be able to sustain the confidence that reliable adults will be available to help them when needed. This has important implications for aftercare, and in particular for the part that foster parents might play in this.

It follows from these principles that adolescents need to be able to experience their foster parents as a secure base from which they may begin to tackle these issues. Members of their foster family need to provide them with opportunities and active encouragement to explore and become confident in the adult world that they are in the process of entering. Foster parents need to support adolescent's efforts to reappraise their relationships with parents and other significant attachment figures without seeking to influence their views or feelings. The foster family also needs to be in a position where they are able to continue to welcome adolescents and young adults back and to support them after the placement ends. This may need to continue until they have consolidated the changes in their internal model of self in relation to attachment figures so that they eventually have a secure base within themselves.

These principles mainly draw attention to the quality of relationship between adolescent and foster family members. They do not cover everything that needs to be considered in order to understand adolescents in foster care, and frameworks for assessment based on them need to be combined with frameworks based on other perspectives. For example assessment based on these principles could be undertaken alongside assessment of an adolescent's developing social, cultural, and racial identity and in relation to changes in particular difficult behaviours.

Once the principles are understood there are a variety of methods that can be used for assessment and intervention. Those that are discussed in Part 3 are not intended to be prescriptive or comprehensive; they are intended to stimulate creative practice and sometimes to indicate that the significance of many practices and techniques that are familiar in current social work practice may be understood and enriched within the framework of attachment theory.

In this chapter the principles that have been outlined will be applied to understanding, assessing and working with adolescents: before a placement starts; in relation to difficulties that develop in the relationship between adolescent and foster parent; through monitoring the progress of the placement, including changes in adolescents' social networks, changes they may wish to make or are making in their relationship to members of their birth family and changes in the way in which they approach and manage negotiations on the boundary between the foster family and the world outside the foster family. The chapter concludes with a consideration of foster parenting as the provision of a secure base from which the adolescent may work on these issues.

Listening to an adolescent before the placement starts: a shared process of assessment and understanding the purpose of the placement

Assessment is not something to be done to adolescents but a process undertaken with them. It is also a continuous process which involves, as far as possible, establishing open communication with the adolescent and listening for emerging issues and themes that will offer clues about the sort of intervention they are likely to find helpful. Once the placement is underway, foster parents will be sharing the task of continuous assessment with social workers and other practitioners.

Preparation for family placement often includes individual work on an adolescent's 'life story' or a preparation group; assessment with the adolescent could be incorporated into such work which has been described well by Ryan and Walker, (1985) and Hapgood, (1988). Alternatively, assessment could be used within a more comprehensive structure for direct work with children such as that devised by Corrigan and Floud, which emphasises the importance of enabling children to be 'in touch with their feelings before helping them to come to terms with them, and with past events'. (Corrigan and Floud, 1990 p. 32.)

Before a placement starts there are likely to be two main purposes in assessment. The first purpose is to establish whether a time limited foster family placement is likely to be an appropriate option for a particular adolescent; whether the adolescent has a reasonably realistic idea of what will be involved for them emotionally, socially and practically and whether they wish to choose this particular route to adulthood. If this is established, then the second purpose is to understand what might be the strengths, vulnerabilities and important issues for this adolescent in relation to the tasks of the placement.

123

When planning for adolescents who are currently being looked after by the local authority, four broad options are likely to be considered: they may return home or to live with another significant attachment figure, they may live in some form of residential care, they may be placed in a new family on a permanent basis, they may be placed in a foster family on a time limited basis. This section starts from the assumption that it has already been established that it is not in the best interests of a particular adolescent to return home or to live with previous carers at this point. It is also based on the assumption that it is totally unacceptable for adolescents to be placed, unaccompanied and unsupported, in bed and breakfast hostels. (Rickford, 1991)

As the study was undertaken in relation to time limited family placements this will remain the focus in this section, with brief references to the other two options of residential care or permanent family placement. The question of whether or not family placement might be a suitable option rests to a large extent on whether a particular adolescent is motivated to risk such an emotionally demanding route into adulthood and whether they are able to envisage with some degree of reality what this will require of them.

In the course of building up a picture of what an adolescent would hope for from family placement, it will help to establish with them what are likely to be their main concerns and preoccupations. The meaning of the placement to the adolescent is of great importance and before a placement starts it is helpful to understand the adolescent's view on why the placement is being offered. Most adolescents looked after by the local authority frame their aims and hopes for the future in terms of relationships; for example, they may wish to get back together with members of their family, make new friends, or experience what it is like to live in a family or they may wish to find and settle down with a partner. They may also have other less personal concerns such as getting on alright at school, doing well in a particular sport, finding work, or getting a place on a college course. Their ideas about having a good time or having fun may appear to be closely linked with real friendships or as an escape from unsatisfactory relationships.

It is useful to consider with them what is the balance between concerns about their relationship with other people and concerns with impersonal activities. An adolescent whose aims are formulated only in impersonal terms or who appears to be envisaging a future that is entirely self sufficient might be able to consider whether this is what they want from life or whether it is what they fear may happen to them if nothing changes for the better. An adolescent whose reasons for wanting a family placement omit any reference to making relationships, and who appears to want to use the foster family's home as they would a hotel room or lodgings is unlikely to be the best candidate for foster care. Within this framework these would be regarded as the most vulnerable adolescents who do still need highly skilled care in a residential setting, where their difficulties in using the care that is available may be recognised and understood.

The balance may also occasionally be weighted in the other direction; before a placement starts the majority of adolescents do not envisage joining another family on a permanent basis, however there are a few who clearly want and need a permanent foster or adoptive placement and it is most important that every effort is made to find them a permanent placement rather than offering them one on a time limited basis.

Assessing an adolescent's inner strengths and vulnerabilities and external resources

The second purpose of assessment before a placement starts is to assess an adolescent's inner strengths and vulnerabilities and external resources, usually in the form of people whose support or companionship is valued, and to anticipate any major difficulties that might be expected in the course of a placement. For example an adolescent may experience herself as resilient, affectionate, and having one or two good friends whom she trusts, but also as moody, liable to do destructive things to herself when life gets her down and having a dreadful temper when she feels she is not being listened to properly, which gets her into a great deal of trouble. She may be concerned that her grandmother, who has always been very important to her, is bitterly opposed to the idea of her living with another family and wonders whether this will involve her in a conflict of loyalty that she will find hard to manage.

125

st assessments draw on a range of theoretical perspectives to ense of very complex data. With adolescents looked after local authority, difficulties often tend to be framed in the particular problem behaviours, such as habitual truancy, stealing, substance abuse, sexual provocation or aggressive outbursts. Identifying these can be helpful as a basis for working out with an adolescent and his or her foster parents appropriate responses and strategies aimed at overcoming them. The particular conceptual framework that is being presented in this book focusses on the adolescent's characteristic patterns of interaction with significant adults and with peers and views many, though not all, problem behaviours as manifestations of a particular pattern of insecure attachment and interaction. Fahlberg suggests that it is useful to consider whether there is a recurrent theme related to attachment that underlie the specific problem behaviours that an adolescent is showing and offers an example of an assessment and case plan based on these ideas. (Fahlberg, 1988, pp. 29-32.)

Before a placement starts, one of the difficulties in assessment may be that an adolescent is not showing any obvious problem behaviours or distorted patterns of attachment at that particular point of time, although they may have been in evidence in the past. It is always tempting to hope that what happened in the past will not happen again, or that past difficulties were entirely due to the adolescent having been the helpless victim of insensitive treatment by previous caregivers. While this may be the case, it is worth bearing in mind an alternative possibility; that this peaceful state of affairs may be because the adolescent is currently in a state akin to 'cold storage' in residential care where they may be experiencing fewer emotional demands on them than will be the case in a family placement lasting for one or two years. It is a good idea for the initial assessment to be reviewed explicitly at intervals throughout the placement. Understanding how an adolescent relates to foster parents, birth parents and other people in his or her social network and the way he or she functions under stress, for example, at entry to a new school, may enable adolescents, foster parents and social workers to anticipate events and issues that are likely to be difficult. It is to the adolescent's relationships within the placement that we now turn.

Understanding the relationship between adolescent and foster parent: patterns of attachment and distance regulation

The adolescents in the study were not subject to existing tests. The method of study combined reports from adolescents and their foster parents on what had been happening during the previous three months of the placement with attention to the interaction between them during the research interviews. Although attempts to relate the behavioural patterns of these adolescents to those found by other researchers in this field have to be tentative, some hypotheses are offered.

It is unlikely that any of the adolescents in this study would have been classified as securely attached had they been tested through the Adult Attachment Interview (George, Kaplan and Main, 1985; Main and Goldwyn, 1989). The adolescents in the study had developed internal working models of self in relation to attachment figures which lead them to perceive adults as unreliable and unavailable when needed. Most adolescents in this study had shorter or longer periods of disorganised behaviour (Main and Hesse, 1990) associated with crises and separations. A few seemed disorganised from start to finish of their placements, which did not last long.

In Chapter 3 it was stated that one way in which internal working models of self in relation to attachment figures may be inferred, was through the adolescent's pattern of emotional and physical distance regulation. Adolescents in the study did not all maintain one pattern of behaviour throughout the placement, most of them showed a mix of behavioural strategies relating to attachment. These strategies were particularly marked in interaction with their foster parents as they crossed and recrossed the family boundary, so that angry or very emotionally detached behaviour was most in evidence around the end of the placement, but also around the transition to school or work and on reunion after a period of going missing. These were described in Chapters 4, 6 and 7.

The three main patterns of attachment in evidence in the study are described below and tentative links made with other researchers' classifications. In the case of adolescents showing each pattern of attachment, the aim of work is stated, some of the tasks defined, and some difficult issues associated with the pattern of behaviour are discussed, drawing on the findings of the study which relate to the interventions by foster parents that adolescents appeared to find helpful or unhelpful.

Anxious attachment

Examples of this pattern would include adolescents who barely let a foster mother out of their sight, or anxiously demand to be accompanied to school, and those whose functioning under stress, for example when trying to get a job, varies in a marked way, depending on the presence of a foster parent or adult child of the family. Andy West's experience of his foster father's support when he was job hunting provides an example of this pattern. Anxious attachment may also show itself in an acute conflict of loyalty between foster parents and previous caregivers, perhaps a grand parent.

The anxiously attached group in this study may correspond with the less insecurely attached subcategories of those preoccupied with attachment or those dismissive of attachment, in the Adult Attachment Interview classification (Main and Goldwyn, 1989). They may also correspond with Hansburg's similarly named category of separation disorder in 11-14 year olds. (Hansburg, 1980a and 1980b).

In Chapter 7 the adolescents whose behaviour was described in Group 1 provide examples of anxious attachment.

To use an analogy, it is as though the adolescent is attached to a life support machine which has to be carried round if he or she is to function adequately.

The aim of work. The aim in interaction with anxiously attached adolescents, is to increase their confidence in the availability and reliability of attachment figures. The evidence that this is happening is that they are able to comfortably increase their distance range from their foster parents and other significant adults and continue to function well under stress as they do so, without at the same time losing their capacity for intimacy and closeness.

128

Tasks. The task here is not to separate adolescents from their attachment figures precipitately, for fear of 'over dependency', but to respond to their need for someone with them under stress. This may involve foster parents moving with adolescents outside the family boundary as they confront stressful situations. An anxiously attached adolescent may only experience the foster family as a secure base if a member of the family is actually there with them at critical times. It is by this means that adults begin to be experienced as potentially reliable and available when they are not physically present. The adolescent needs to be the one to take the initiative to move further away and be more independent. This was well illustrated in the range of interaction concerned with negotiating the transition to school or work.

Once an alliance has been formed between adolescent and foster family members, it is likely to prove helpful if they join forces with teachers, employers, members of the adolescent's birth family, social workers etc. to enable the adolescent to function well under stress in an arena outside the foster home. It is unhelpful if a foster parent appears to form an alliance, say with a teacher, before first forming an alliance with the adolescent.

Difficult issues. Attention, empathy and acceptance may prove problematic for some foster parents when adolescents are anxiously attached to a birth parent or grandparent. It may be hard for a foster parent to understand why an adolescent is constantly running off home, either when they are in difficulties themselves, or to check that their relative has not been taken ill, succumbed to some crisis or even died in their absence; in chapter 6, Lee Robinson provides an example of this behaviour. It is essential that foster parents appreciate the adolescent's concerns and take them seriously, otherwise the conflict of loyaly will become intolerable for the adolescent. Sometimes foster parents find themselves able to take on some of the caring for birth parents, thus relieving the adolescent of this burden.

When an adolescent is anxiously attached to a foster parent, allowing for the degree of contact and support that he or she appears to be needing, flies in the face of traditional practice wisdom which says 'he's got to learn' by such practices as turning a paralysed, job hunting adolescent out of the house and refusing entry until meal times as happened to Frank Little, who was described in Chapter 4.

The concern is that anxiously attached adolescents will not change sufficiently fast on their own initiative in the course of a time limited placement. Yet the evidence from the study suggests that it is anxiously attached adolescents who fare best and are able to become increasingly self reliant in placements where foster parents are prepared to accompany them to stressful encounters in the early stages of the placement. Standing alongside an adolescent in the belief that by doing this they really will be enabled to function adequately themselves, often requires a considerable act of faith. It is much more emotionally demanding than doing everything for them or doing nothing for them or even than telling them what to do.

Hostile, ambivalent attachment

Examples of this pattern were seen in a number of adolescent girls who went missing, such as Gina Fitzgerald and Dawn Gibson described in Chapter 6. These adolescents seem to oscillate to and fro, away from the foster home and back. Sometimes this involves splitting a 'bad' foster family and a 'good' outside person and then reversing the split.

Although great care has to be taken when comparing the behaviour of adolescents with that of much younger children the group of girls described as hostile and ambivalent in this study appear to show behaviour that has some similarities to Crittenden's (1985) A/C classification of maltreated infants. This group corresponded closely with Hansburg's category of hostile anxious attachment.

In Chapter 7, adolescents whose behaviour was described in Group 3 provide examples of this behaviour.

To return to the analogy of the life support machine, it is as though the adolescent is engaged in a constant process of sawing through the connection with the life support machine and then frantically trying to repair it. The repair is usually temporary and becomes increasingly difficult to effect over time.

Bowlby's concept of dysfunctional anger (Bowlby, 1973, pp. 248-251) is helpful in making sense of this process. The adolescent's anger may have originally been functional in an attempt to recall or recover an absent parent, but when it is repeatedly acted out in a new relationship, it has the opposite effect of weakening the bonds it sought to strengthen.

The aim of work. The aim in interaction with adolescents showing a hostile, angry pattern of attachment is to reduce the oscillating pattern of going missing and returning.

Tasks. Provision of a secure base when an adolescent shows this pattern of behaviour involves maintaining a consistent stance, without recrimination, and continuing to be available and to 'welcome back' each time the adolescent is ready to make the reconnection with the life support machine, as occurs when an adolescent returns from going missing.

Helpful feedback to the adolescent is likely to involve a considerable amount of limit setting and straight setting out of consequences of behaviour. It is in this way that unhelpful, collusive, escalating hostility is likely to be avoided, in which foster parents find themselves sucked into the adolescent's pattern of hostile interaction, saying and doing things they regard as totally out of character and subsequently bitterly regret. This was illustrated in Chapter 6 in the account of the interaction between Gina Fitzgerald and the Hendersons.

Difficult issues. After an initial period of pursuit and bringing home missing adolescents, the next stage may involve the foster home becoming an arena for their angry behaviour. This may well be even more trying for the foster parents, as Mrs Hatton's description in Chapter 7 of this phase in her work with Dawn Gibson, illustrates. After the period when Dawn repeatedly spent nights out following the fair, with Mrs Hatton in hot pursuit, Dawn started breaking into the foster home and stealing Mrs Hatton's belongings.

Here the need is for foster parents to separate their objective reaction to the incident, whether it be anger or distress, from their own past personal experience. This may involve foster parents giving straight feedback on their reaction to destructive behaviour, for example, in Chapter 2, in the way the Armstrongs told Tom, that they felt like taking him out and throttling him when he furiously rejected their efforts to help him get to work. If foster parents do not express their reaction to the adolescent's behaviour then and there, the situation is likely to escalate. Such interaction is also important for demonstrating to adolescents that their behaviour has consequences in the real world.

If everyone manages to weather this turbulent phase, there is greater likelihood of adolescents becoming more reflective about their own behaviour, anticipating danger points, finding alternative strategies, and recognising that the anger is misdirected. If this is to come about, it will be through foster parents' own reflective stance and their resistance to being sucked into adolescents' pattern of hostile interaction.

In Chapter 10 there is further discussion about the task for social workers and other practitioners in relation to escalating anger between adolescent and foster parent.

Emotionally detached behaviour

This pattern of behaviour involves emotional distancing, and sometimes physical distancing, either by going missing, or by retreating physically within the household. These adolescents are often quite isolated, and have more difficulty than others with making new friends when they move to a foster family. Within this pattern of interaction two main variations emerge.

The first sub-group are low in self reliance, they tend to be passive, compliant, and have difficulty taking the initiative. They give little feedback to their foster parents about how they are experiencing the placement, particularly whether they feel it is worthwhile, or whether anyone in the foster family holds any significance for them. Equally, outside the foster home they show little evidence of functioning very well but seem unable to use help from other people to manage better.

The second sub-group show a high level of self sufficiency, especially when away from the foster home. They are fiercely self reliant, and sometimes precipitate the end of the placement in order to gain their independence. They are likely to be competent survivors in adult life, but without intimate relationships.

The behaviour of the group of boys in this study described as emotionally detached showed the clearest organisation and would appear to correspond to adults classified through the Adult Attachment Interview and Kobak and Sceery's group of late adolescents who are dismissive of attachment (George, Kaplan and Main, 1985; Kobak and Sceery; 1988; Main and Goldwyn, 1989). This group of emotionally detached boys probably included the categories identified by Hansburg showing hostile detachment, dependent detachment and excessive self sufficiency (Hansburg, 1980a and 1980b).

In Chapter 7 adolescents in Group 2 provide examples of this behaviour.

Within this group it is as though their awareness of the life support machine has been blunted or deactivated. It has been disconnected and the task for them and their foster parents is to find ways of reconnecting it.

The aim of work. The aim of interaction with adolescents showing a pattern of emotionally detached behaviour is to encourage and enable the adolescent to test themselves out in less distanced interaction. The initiative to move closer needs to come from them, but foster parents can help the process by careful attention to the adolescent's cues. There is evidence from the study that sensitive and accurate responses at these critical points do help to shift adolescents towards a closer relationship with their foster parents, the Armstrong's work with Tom Skipper provided many instances of this. There is also evidence for the contrary process where cues were missed.

Tasks. Establishing a secure base is a very difficult task with this group, particularly with those who are passive and show little self reliance. Those who are fiercely self reliant may distance themselves and then begin to negotiate for a secure base from a safe distance. Christine Faber, described in Chapters 4 and 6, provides a good example of this in the way that she was unable to sustain her alliance with her foster mother when she was job hunting; she went missing, found work, and was subsequently able to use her foster mother as a secure base, first by phone, and later by returning for a successful placement.

Difficult issues. Foster parents find it difficult to go on attending to and empathising with adolescents showing emotionally detached behaviour. Lack of feedback from adolescents makes it hard for foster parents to believe that they are offering anything of value and in turn when adolescents do make a real contribution to planning their future, their foster parents may find it difficult to hear this or take it seriously. This was well illustrated in Chapters 5 and 7 with Ben Little, in relation to Ben trying to establish a home base with his brothers.

With adolescents showing emotionally detached patterns of behaviour there is a great temptation for foster parents to form an alliance with other caregivers and professionals before forming an alliance with the adolescent, who then feels excluded and may in turn exclude themselves from the placement. The aim here is to reduce the adolescent's emotional distancing achieved through physically moving to and fro between the people concerned and keeping life in totally separate compartments.

Understanding the progress of the placement

Adolescents' current patterns of relating to their foster parents will have grown out of their experiences with their birth families and other previous caregivers and will, in turn influence their current relationship with members of their social network, and the progress they make in the placement. A useful way to start to assess their progress is to chart their changing social network.

Charting the changing social network

One criterion for a successful placement is that there should be a degree of open, explicit agreement between adolescent and foster parent about the purposes and significance of the placement. This presupposes that the adolescent is able to sustain a sense of how he or she wishes to use the placement and about internal and external changes taking place as the placement progresses. Adolescents who experience their lives and relationships as fragmented, particularly those who have experienced a series of placements, may be helped by relatively simple exercises that enable them to take stock of their social network and to monitor changes in their relation to the people in this network as the placement progresses. As stated earlier, the references to particular techniques that follow, many of which will be familiar, are intended as suggestions and as spurs to practitioners' own creativity. They may be used with adolescents preparing for placement or at intervals through the placement as a form of monitoring or review.

A starting point is for adolescent and social worker or foster parent to work together on who an adolescent has been in touch with over a specified period, such as the last week, month or three months. The length of time chosen needs to be long enough to encompass most of the people that the adolescent is in touch with. For an adolescent who has been highly unsettled, following a series of rapid moves through placements, a shorter time span may prove more manageable.

It is helpful for these contacts to be plotted diagramatically by the adolescent, for example, in the form of an eco chart (Fahlberg 1981a), or network map or less permanently, through arranging small candles representing each person in the adolescent's network on a tray around a central candle representing the adolescent. The initial aim is to provide an opportunity for an adolescent to identify the people, places, and activities that feature in their day to day lives, as well as identifying people who are important to them and who they feel that they have lost touch with or do not see very often. It is helpful to find a way of charting how much contact they have had with a particular person over a specified period as this may well change over the course of a placement and in itself can be useful tool for exploring with the adolescent the meaning of such changes.

The contrast in the network maps drawn by different adolescents or in network maps drawn by the same adolescent at intervals through a placement can be very striking. This exercise, in itself, without exploration of the adolescents feelings about the people they have identified is often revealing; some adolescents are in touch with many members of a large extended family. In contrast others may have had no contact with anyone outside their current placement other than their social worker and school. Some will draw network maps which show contact with a range of institutions but indicate few, if any, intimate relationships. Exercises such as those using candles provide powerful metaphors which an adolescent may be able to use to make sense of what is happening to them and and then begin to communicate what it is that they would like to happen during the placement (Heard, personal communication).

Without necessarily developing such an exercise further it may be a useful one to repeat at intervals through the placement as a means of charting changes and developments. It is likely to show the extent to which the adolescent has been integrated into the foster family's existing network of relatives and friends and the extent to which the adolescent is closely in touch with birth family or friends. For adolescents who are not able to be in touch with more than a very restricted range of feelings about the people in their lives, it can provide a non-threatening way in to reflecting on their relationships.

A map of a social network may also be used as a basis for further exploration of how adolescents feel about their birth parents and other people in their network. Whom do they experience as providing support, caregiving and/or companionability? Whom do they feel angry with? Whom do they experience as criticising or rejecting them? Does any pattern emerge of how they experience themselves and others in close relationships?

Many adolescents in care have been forced into the position of 'parental children' as a means of getting some care for themselves from their parents. If so, they may find it difficult to seek out companions or attachment figures directly, instead they find that relating to others as a caregiver is a safer option than seeking care for themselves in a direct manner. A picture may emerge of an adolescent who has strong, perhaps quite mixed feelings for people in his or her network, or alternatively a picture where there is little real differentiation and a certain flatness in the way current relationships are described.

Understanding adolescents' appraisal of their birth family and other significant caregivers

Information and understanding about who are an adolescent's attachment figures, and how an adolescent views them can only be gained in full partnership with the adolescent, in order to avoid either making unwarranted assumptions about who is or is not important, or missing significant people out completely. We need to know how realistic they are able to be about these relationships, for example, do they idealise their relationship with a parent when the evidence provides a less benign picture? Does their anger about the way someone has treated them, currently preclude them from any wider reflection on what has happened?

136

Much is being learned from the use of recently devised instruments and in particular the Adult Attachment Inte (Main, Kaplan and Cassidy, 1985; Main, 1991), about significance of the coherence with which adults and adolescents recall and recount their early memories of interaction with their parents and other attachment figures. An adolescent may be helped to move on from a generalised description of their early relationship with a parent or other attachment figure to more particular memories by first being asked for words that would describe that relationship; 'warm' or 'harsh' for example, and then being asked for particular memories of themselves and their parent together that would illustrate that description. Further detailed memories can sometimes be triggered by asking what the adolescent remembers doing when they were emotionally upset, physically hurt or ill. To whom did they turn? What response did they get? For some adolescents, memories will be of turning away or avoiding contact with adults when they were upset and nursing their wounds alone. Questions could also be asked about how they remember reacting to early separations, threats of abandonment or feelings of rejection.

In this way a picture may be built up, not only of the specific experiences they have had, but also of their current position in relation to those experiences. Some people whose early experiences have been harsh are able to give a coherent account of events and experiences and be in touch with the feelings associated with these events. Evidence suggests that they have been successful in unlinking themselves from earlier inner working models of self in relation to attachment figures and are able to form secure attachments in the present. Others tend to idealise their parents but find it difficult to recall specific memories of care which would support this or even to recall childhood memories at all. Their accounts may be excessively succinct. As adults or adolescents they may be dismissive of attachment. In contrast, others offer long, rambling accounts that are full of contradictions and indicate that they are still highly preoccupied with these early relationships. Some may make highly implausible statements regarding the causes and consequences of loss and other traumatic events. These may have be experiencing unresolved feelings about a significant traumatic experience.

social task of reappraising relationships may be
relation to parents, siblings, grandparents, or non-
ers, and sometimes a combination of these. As well
discover, explore and come to terms with their
ese people, they are likely to need to test out their
ity as potential providers of a home base. For
oked after by the local authority the process of
reappraisal is very often a painful one, both for them and for those
who work with them, as it may involve a powerful mix of anger,
grief and disillusionment.

The danger for professionals working closely with adolescents
is that they allow their own feelings about the adolescent's birth
family and other previous carers to guide them into persuasive
pronouncements about whom they regard as desirable or
undesirable people for the adolescent to make his home with when
the placement ends. However clear the outcome may seem to the
adults concerned, it is essential that adolescents make their own
discoveries. One implication is that planning and initial agreements
about the purpose of the placement may need to be left open ended
as to where older adolescents will live at the end of the placement.
Within the context of the external constraints, such as whether
there is a home for them to return to, part of the agenda for
placements may be for adolescents to reach their own position on
this. This presupposes that a real alternative home base will be
available, and that work with the adolescent's birth family and
perhaps between the adolescent and his or her family is also
happening.

Whether a foster parent or social worker is the best person to
undertake direct work with the adolescent concerning his birth
family or other previous care givers is best decided on the basis of
which arrangement seems most comfortable for all concerned in a
particular placement.

*Understanding behaviour related to the psychosocial tasks of
adolescence*

Assessing the impact of various hazardous events. The various
psychosocial tasks involved in the transition into adult life come
within Caplan's (1964) definition of a hazardous event, that is an
event involving, or with the potential for creating, disequilibrium

or discontinuity in the life space or assumptive world of the person concerned. In Chapter 3 it was suggested that these events often constituted the junction points in a person's developmental pathway, which might converge or diverge further from an optimal course, depending on how they were negotiated. They frequently cause great anxiety and it is helpful to have as clear a picture as possible of the way an adolescent has reacted to previous important transitions or crises, particularly those involving separation or loss as this may give clues to particular vulnerabilities or strengths. Equally, the way an adolescent negotiates with foster parents on the boundary between the family and the world outside the family, such as the transition to school or work at the beginning of a placement, often provides an indicator of the way they may approach other hazardous events later in the placement.

By identifying and reviewing with an adolescent the impact on them of earlier critical events, it is possible to explore how they negotiated these events at the time, how they perceive and feel about them now and what might be the implications or special help they might need if they are to negotiate the transition to adult life successfully. For example, in Chapter 2, Tom Skipper's account of his early life, losses and series of moves in care presents a picture of a child who reacted to hazardous events by dissociating himself from many of the painful feelings they must have engendered. In the present, however, in an apparently unimportant episode when Mr Armstrong upset Tom's routine for getting to work, Tom experienced revengeful anger. On the basis of this assessment it might have been possible to anticipate that when it came to major hazardous events, such as the end of the placement, Tom would be likely to have difficulty in staying in touch with his anger. If so, appropriate action could have been taken to encourage him to express his anger more directly with his foster parents. It is possible that this would have reduced the extent of his delinquency and probable that it would have helped Tom keep in better touch with the Armstrongs once the placement ended.

Understanding the significance of adolescents' current behaviour for later developments in the placement. In the same way that an understanding about reactions to earlier transitions and crises may provide indicators for difficulties or vulnerabilities within the

139

placement, continuous assessment of interaction with foster parents on the boundary between the family and the world outside the family during the placement may provide similar indicators. For example, findings from the study, discussed in Chapter 4, indicated that the way the transition to new school or work was managed often had predictive value for the course the placement would subsequently take. Consequently a difficulty identified at this point could alert practitioners to the possibility that all was not well and extra help could be offered. It was clear that the common factor for the majority of adolescents in care when facing these difficult negotiations on the boundary between the family and the wider world, was their extremely high levels of anxiety as shown in their expectation of failure, and there tendency to flight or immobility. Past experiences led them very rapidly to expect that their worst fears would be realised.

Beyond this general observation, the particular starting point may vary greatly and needs to be assessed. In practice the transition to new school or work at the beginning of the placement provides a crucial opportunity for foster parents to establish a strong alliance with the adolescent and where this happens it frequently appears to have an important influence on the subsequent course of the placement. At this point the social worker's most helpful role is firstly to facilitate foster parents' links with school, careers service or employers. Secondly, social workers need to help foster parents make sense of what the adolescent may be asking for from them. This is especially valuable when the adolescent's signals may be distorted and difficult to recognise, such as defiantly maintaining 'I'm not bothered', or despairing that they will ever be offered a job 'when they know you're in care'. Thirdly, social workers need to encourage foster parents to take on the role of helping adolescents into school or work, and if appropriate, accompanying them to difficult encounters and being ready to talk these through afterwards. This important role for the social worker, working at one remove from the adolescent, will be discussed in Chapter 10.

Assessing adolescents' relationships with their peers. Although peer relationships have not been the focus of this study, it is important that they should be included in an assessment of adolescents' networks and more particularly of their attachment relationships if we are to have a rounded picture of the manner in which they are making their way in the world. Peer relationships are considered briefly here because an adolescent's peers are often expected to be an important source of support when times are difficult. When seeking to evaluate the significance of peer relationships it is worth bearing in mind an implication of some recent studies which suggests that the importance of peers for offering attachment relationships in adolescence should not be over estimated.

Greenberg, Siegel and Leitch (1983) in a study of 12-19 year olds found that while the quality of perceived attachments both to parents and peers was related to well-being, the quality of attachment to parents was significantly more powerful than that to peers in predicting well being and as an effective buffer against the effects of negative and stressful experience. Hodges and Tizard (1989) comparing a population of 16 year old ex-institutional adolescents with a control group found that the ex-institutional adolescents were more likely to have difficulties with their peers, were less likely to have a special friend, were less likely to see their peers as a source of emotional support, and were more oriented to adult attention and approval. One-fifth appeared to be friendly to any peer rather than choosing friends. These studies suggest that it is unusual for peer relationships in adolescence to compensate fully for insecure attachments to adults.

Through a discussion of an adolescent's peer relationships it may also be possible to assess the extent to which they are able to develop sexually intimate friendships and the extent to which they express their sexuality in ways that are defensively cut off from companionable interaction. (Heard and Lake 1986)

Foster parenting as the provision of a secure base for exploration

So far the focus has been on understanding adolescents within a network of relationships. In this final section we draw together the threads in relation to what a foster parent needs to offer in order to work with an adolescent effectively in a time limited placement. It has been the argument of this book that if adolescents in care are to develop their capacity for relationships of mature interdependence in adult life, they require a form of parenting which enables them

141

to experience those who care for them as a secure base for exploration. By this means they will be enabled to move out into adult life with greater confidence in their own personal resources and those of other people who they can rely on to be available when the need arises.

Winnicott used the term 'holding' to describe a mother's adaptation to her infant's moods, needs and communications in the interests of his or her emotional growth and development. Inadvertently, because of its associations with infancy the term has sometimes led people to the misleading impression that such sensitive responsiveness to the needs of older children and adolescents who were deprived of this quality of care as infants or young children will result in them becoming permanently stuck in a dependent relationship with their caregivers.

For a child or an adult to change from a pattern of making insecure attachments to making more secure attachments, they will need to experience a particular quality of secure caregiving. This may be offered by an adult partner or friend, a therapist or social worker or, as this book has aimed to show, by foster parents. Earlier in this chapter, there has been some brief discussion of research evidence which links an adult's position in relation to attachment, parenting style and infant and young children's pattern of attachment, thus enabling us to understand more about intergenerational transmission of attachment patterns (Main, Kaplan and Cassidy. 1985; Ricks, 1985).

Whether considering the dyad or the family, one of the important contributions made by attachment theory is to challenge the notion that empathy and sensitive responsiveness to the attachment behaviour of insecurely attached people will inevitably result in them becoming permanently dependent, and unable to shoulder adult responsibilities. In recasting the idea of 'holding' in terms of attachment theory, Heard argues that it is possible to consider the family

> as a homeostatic system of relationships between individuals at different stages of development who share set goals aimed at terminating a specific form of proximity-seeking attachment behaviour and promoting exploratory behaviour. (Heard, 1978, p. 67)

In other words, the experience of attachment behaviour being assuaged frees a person's capacity for emotional and social development. It follows from this that the purpose and likely outcome of foster family members developing reliable, consistent alliances with adolescents in their care is not that they should engender overdependency, but that this is the way in which adolescents' requests for help will be recognised and met. By this means they will be encouraged to manage their own lives confidently, and build up experience of other people coming to their aid when they need them. Some of the ways in which relationships between foster parents, their own children and fostered adolescents may help or hinder this process are discussed in Chapters 9 and 10. The components of parental behaviour, as understood within this framework, will now be considered in relation to foster parents' work with adolescents in their care.

Care-taking

In general terms, the primary goal of parental behaviour is to respond to the child's requests for proximity when he/she seeks it and until he/she is ready to resume exploration and move further away. With adolescents displaying disordered patterns of attachment behaviour, their foster parents' ability to respond to this with an appropriate combination of physical proximity and empathy has a similar function.

This task often proves to be a complex one for foster parents caring for very insecurely attached adolescents as it may be more difficult for them to recognise when an adolescent wants a foster parent actually alongside them or to be sure how much intimacy they can tolerate. This is because the cues may be distorted or be communicated angrily; alternatively, wishes for attachment to a foster parent may have become confusingly entangled with bids for sexual intimacy as a result of previous experience of sexually abusive relationships with other adults.

A foster parent's responsiveness involves staying in touch with the adolescent's agenda and goals, even when these differ from or are in conflict with their own, or are justifiably regarded as undesirable. In order to do this, the purposes and significance of the placement need to be shared openly and explicitly with the adolescent, even at the risk of conflict. This aspect of parenting presented difficulties to a number of foster parents in the study and will be considered further in Chapter 10 in relation to ways in which foster parents may be enabled to work effectively.

Timing and pacing of interventions are often crucial, the art is knowing when to keep still and when to intervene. Foster parents who are not carrying with them a great deal of fury, frustration and hurt from their own childhood experiences are more likely to intervene in ways which are sensitively responsive to the adolescent. However the experience of being the recipient of an adolescent's distorted perception, for example, that their foster parents 'wants nothing better than to see them behind bars' points to the need for all foster parents to have someone outside the family on whom they can rely. This person's task is to enable the foster parent to sort out what belongs to the present from what is being carried over from the past in their relationship with an adolescent, and in the adolescent's relationship with them.

Feedback

The process of verbal feedback to the adolescent relating to the impact of their behaviour and what are the likely consequences of it, becomes an important way of challenging obsolete internal working models of self as a helpless victim of circumstances, or as totally unlikeable. This is well illustrated in the Armstrong's work with Tom Skipper and Andy West described in Chapters 2, 4 and 5. This style of feedback which is straight, unambiguous and leaves the responsibility for change with the adolescent is likely to be the most effective form of limit setting with this age group.

The foster parents' work with Tom and Andy also shows ways in which feedback in the form of constructive reformulation of thoughts and feelings may became part of the process which enables an adolescent to explore, reflect upon and test out their relationships with members of their birth family and other previous significant caregivers, where previously this had been avoided for fear of being overwhelmed by their strength of feeling. It was by this means that these adolescents were able to come to their own reappraisal of themselves in relation to their attachment figures and to become clearer about the nature of the contact that they would like with them in future.

Heard (1978) argues that it is in the context of a reliable alliance that exploration and reappraisal of predictions about self and others may take place. An alliance has most chance of developing when foster parents are able to combine sensitive caregiving and well timed feedback. The alliance between adolescent and foster parent becomes the context within which obsolete internal working models of self in relation to attachment figures are challenged and change for the better takes place.

This challenge essentially involves open emotional communication on the part of foster parents in their relationship with an adolescent in their care. Bretherton,(1990b) has reviewed studies linking caregiver sensitivity, communication patterns and internal working models. These include two types of study; the first type contrasts the communication patterns of secure and insecure dyads within attachment relationships; so far these studies have concerned infant-parent and toddler-parent attachments. The second type of study focusses on how a person, whether child or adult, communicates about attachment relationships.

> Secure relationships, it turns out, go hand in hand with the partners' ability to engage in emotionally open, fluent, and coherent communication, both within attachment relationships and about attachment relationships. Insecure relationships, by contrast, seem to be characterized by selective ignoring of signals, as well as by certain forms of incoherence and dysfluency when discussing attachment relationships. (Bretherton, 1990b, p.58)

A foster parent who is able to offer this quality of open emotional communication is likely to enable an insecurely attached adolescent to put into words, their thoughts, perceptions, and feelings about their relationship with significant people in their lives. In adolescence, this reflective process, shared with trusted people, is likely to be a critical part of challenging obsolete internal working models of self in relation to attachment figures. It is particularly unfortunate when an adolescent who has great difficulty communicating coherently about his relationship with his birth family is placed with a foster family who appear to have similar difficulties in discussing openly and coherently with the adolescent, this all important aspect of his or her life.

This concept of parenting as offering a secure base for exploration may be compared and contrasted with the concept of behavioral parenting outlined by Hazel(1981) and Shaw and Hipgrave (1983), and the concept of psychological parenting which they criticise as inappropriate in relation to adolescent fostering. It has similarities with behavioral parenting in its focus on aspects of behaviour, such as distance regulation and communication. It differs from behavioural parenting in its emphasis on the need for reliable relationships which are continuous over a period of months or years and in relation to which the adolescent feels he or she has some responsibility for negotiating the timing and manner of its ending. It is similar to psychological parenting in its emphasis on the importance of foster parents' empathy and sensitive responsiveness to need. It differs from psychological parenting in its proposition that parenting behaviour that offers a secure base for exploration to adolescents, does not necessarily involve foster parents becoming permanent or primary attachment figures, and indeed must avoid getting into a rivalrous position of needing to be a better parent than birth parents or other earlier attachment figures. It may also be thought of in terms of the whole family taking on this function, and this is particularly apt in families whose young adult children are involved with the placement.

Summary

In the light of this chapter we now have an understanding of what adolescent fostering may be expected to achieve and how it is likely to acheive it. The criteria against which these achievements may be assessed are:

1. Is the adolescent able to make progress in negotiating the transition to adult life? This involves considering their approach to particular psychosocial tasks such as making friends, finding work or using educational opportunities, renegotiating relationships with members of his or her birth family and other previous attachment figures, and moving out

146

to establish a base of their own. This may be summarised as progress in negotiating with confidence across the family boundary and using the help offered by foster family members as they do so, as illustrated in the key events discussed in Part 2.

2. Is the adolescent able to experience and use the foster home as a secure base for developing greater flexibility in their pattern of attachment and distance regulation? This will provide evidence for changes in their internal model of self in relation to attachment figures.

3. Is the adolescent able to reappraise earlier relationships, and reach a realistic appraisal of current relationships with members of their birth family and other important attachment figures?

In order that these achievements may be realised it is necessary to consider the following questions in relation to a placement:

1. Do adolescent and foster parent agree sufficiently about the purpose of the placement?

2. To what extent are the purposes and significance of the placement as perceived by adolescent and foster family members shared openly and explicitly between them? When purposes are in conflict, are they able to agree to differ?

3. Have adolescent and foster parents developed a mutually satisfying relationship? This tends to be associated with continued contact between adolescent and foster family members when the placement ends. A mutually unsatisfactory relationship tends to be associated with no contact between adolescent and foster family members when the placement ends.

The task of the placement is to enable adolescents to negotiate the transition to adult life successfully. They will be helped in doing so if they are able to increase their capacity for making trusting relationships with adults and peers and to manage more flexibly the way they regulate physical and emotional distance between themselves and others. An important part of this process is likely to involve their reappraisal of relationships with earlier attachment figures and renegotiation of their position in relation

147

to them. Particular attention needs to be paid to the way in which adolescents manage critical or potentially hazardous events as this may provide indicators of future vulnerabilities and strengths, and help be offered accordingly.

In order to fulfill the tasks of the placement successfully, a form of parenting is required which both contains anxiety and supports exploration and risk taking. This is described as foster parents providing the adolescent with a secure base for exploration. In the light of this, we now turn to consider the foster family as a whole.

9 Assessing and working with foster families

The focus so far in Part 3 has been on assessing and understanding the interaction between fostered adolescents and their foster parents and it has been concerned with the foster parent/adolescent dyad. While the emphasis has been mainly on identifying and understanding characteristic patterns of attachment and distance regulation which adolescents bring to family placements, it has also offered a conceptual model of parenting for adolescents and described the some of the main skills that contribute to this approach to the fostering task.

The focus in this chapter shifts to understanding variations in family functioning which will influence foster parents' response. Part of the process of assessing families who are interested in offering placements to adolescents who are looked after by the local authority and in subsequent collaborative work with them, involves recognising and understanding patterns of attachment and caregiving in individual family members, in subsystems and in the whole family system. This chapter is mainly concerned with the foster family as a system, but in order to move from a consideration of the way adolescent and foster parent interact as a dyad to consider the dynamic implications of a fostered adolescent joining a new family system, some bridges must first be built.

The foundations for bridge building were laid at the end of Chapter 3 where Heard's concept of the attachment dynamic

(Heard 1978, 1982) and other related concepts were introduced. Heard describes the attachment dynamic as follows

> The dynamic provides a working model to explain the extent to which the complementary activities of attachment behaviour and care-giving behaviour (a) govern the movements of family members towards and away from each other; (b) affect the degree to which they each engage in creative exploratory activities; and (c) influence the internal representations each family member builds of him or herself in action with others or when acting alone. It is suggested that it is the operation of the dynamic that makes it appear as though they constitute a more, or less, open system. (Heard, 1982, p. 101)

This model also provides a way of linking the attachment, caregiving and exploratory behaviour of individual family members, with behaviours operating within subsystems of the family, as well as those operating in the whole family system. The individual foster parent's current position in respect to experiences and feelings relating to attachment will first be considered, followed by a consideration of aspects of the attachment dynamic as it operates in the parent-child and sibling subsystems, and what may happen when new alliances form when an adolescent joins the family. Finally, aspects of the functioning of the whole family system will be considered and related to the needs of adolescents whose relationships are characterised by different patterns of attachment. Some general comments on working with foster families during the assessment period serve as an introduction.

The process of assessment with foster families

As with adolescents, the process of assessment is not something to be done to families but a process undertaken with them. The adult members are invited to consider, amongst other things, their own attachment history and some of the ways in which it might have bearing on their present parenting of their own children and their future work as foster parents. It is sometimes argued that it is unnecessary, even unhelpful for families offering to foster to be encouraged to become more consciously aware of the way that they operate as a family and as individual family members. However, while it may be possible to work for much of the time at an intuitive level, self-awareness is likely to extend the range of situations in which foster parents and social workers are able to respond constructively and avoid behaviour which hinders adolescents from changing to more flexible and appropriate patterns of relating.

The process of assessment, is likely to involve work between family members, between a social worker and individual family members, with the marital and parental subsystem, and possibly the sibling subsystem and with the whole family. It is also helpful to include discussion in foster parent groups. For example, in preparation and support groups, members of different foster families will implicitly be comparing different styles of operating. An advantage of making these styles more explicit within the group is to emphasise that within a broad range of functioning, foster parents can be effective and helpful to a range of adolescents in care. If foster parents are able to become more aware of the way they operate, it will help them clarify which adolescents they are most likely to be able to work with effectively and to be aware of situations they may find particularly difficult.

Initially the emphasis will be on assessment, including self-assessment during the preparatory and training periods, culminating in a formal decision whether or not to approve a family for placement. However assessment is a continuing process if social workers, with the families concerned, are to go on learning about a family's strengths and areas of vulnerability in work with a range of adolescents. Although the demand for family placements frequently precludes attempts at matching adolescents and families, on the occasions where this is possible, a framework for assessment along certain dimensions provides a basis for matching. Some of the implications of matching adolescents with families, in relation to their respective patterns of attachment and caregiving are discussed later in this chapter.

There are a number of potential hazards in offering criteria for assessing foster families. One hazard is that the criteria could be used to exclude all but a few families who approximate to an ideal. Equally, however they may be used to exclude a few, but in most cases to identify strengths or weaknesses in families for a particular type of fostering and to focus help and support where it is most likely to be needed. Another hazard in offering criteria based on one theoretical perspective is that of developing a narrowed vision such that particular dimensions of family functioning, in this case those concerned with attachment and caregiving, are considered to be all that needs to be assessed. The dimensions of family functioning that are discussed in this chapter are not exclusive, they need to be used in conjunction with the general literature on assessment of families for child placement, and particular formats for family description such as the BAAF Form F. or the Summary Format of Family Functioning, which have been designed to encompass a range of theoretical perspectives (Bingley et al., 1984).

Assessing attachment history and a foster parent's position in relation to attachment

While there is general acceptance of the idea that foster parents' experiences of their own childhood and parenting is likely to affect their approach to fostering significantly, it is not always obvious what sense to make of the account they offer. Some people who report very adverse circumstances in their own upbringing appear to be able to use their experience as a resource in caring for difficult adolescents, while for others a history involving apparently less adversity still acts as a constraint to their capacity as caregivers. It is not so much what has happened to a person as their ability to integrate all aspects of their past experience, including the strong feelings attached to those experiences which affects their current caregiving behaviour. The difficulty most of us have in assimilating and integrating past experience results in a widespread tendency to filter out certain aspects of our early experience, so that quite unintentionally we give an account that may be idealised or very partial or devoid of the feelings that were originally associated with the events.

A recently developed research interview, the Berkeley Adult Attachment Interview, was discussed briefly in Chapter 8. Some of the findings from research using this instrument are repeated and discussed here with particular reference to implications for assessing foster parents. It suggests that the manner in which a person narrates their history of attachment, separation and loss, provides indications of their current position in relation to attachment. The interview is designed to

> probe alternately for descriptions of relationships, specific supportive memories, contradictory memories, assessments of relationships in childhood, and current assessments of the same experiences and relationships.(Main and Goldwyn, 1984, p. 211)

Although the process involved in analysing the interview for research purposes is likely to be too complex to make it readily useable for assessing foster parents, it suggests a number of indicators of an adult's current state of mind regarding attachment. These indicators would be recognisable to a social worker focussing with a prospective foster parent on their early history, including their feelings for and experiences with their own parents and other caregivers. For both parents, their current position regarding attachment has been found to relate to the security of attachment of their own children and for the mother, this relationship is strong (Main and Goldwyn, 1984; Main, Kaplan and Cassidy,1985; Main, 1991).

Adults who are currently secure in relation to attachment experiences value past and present attachment relationships, and are objective in the way they describe particular early relationships, not idealising them. Their account is likely to be coherent, with an ease of recall, a development of ideas and a readiness to integrate the positive and negative aspects of expression and feeling. In contrast, the information given by parents of insecure children often seems unintegrated, and may include contradictions, inconsistencies, and distortions. For example, they might describe a parent's relationship with them when they were young as 'excellent' or 'loving', but later in the interview when asked to recall particular events, they might offer an illustration which indicates failures of parenting. Sometimes the account seems disorganised, with the person being interviewed losing track of the question or topic, or apparently unconnected matters are introduced which interrupt the flow of ideas. Sometimes information seems 'closed off', the subject cannot remember certain periods in his or her past.

It seems reasonable to assume that foster parents who are having difficulty integrating their own positive and negative experiences of attachment are likely to be hampered in their efforts to stay in touch with sufficient sensitivity and objectivity to the messages underlying an adolescents' distorted pattern of attachment behaviour. While all is going well for the adolescent, foster parents may appear to be managing reasonably well, but when presented with difficult behaviour, they are more likely to experience this as a hostile attack or rejection. When this happens their own attachment behaviour may be activated, temporarily overriding their caregiving capacity and they find themselves unable to work creatively with what is being presented to them.

Foster parents' own children

The nature of the interaction between a fostered adolescent and children of the family appears to have an important influence on whether the placement is experienced as safe enough for the adolescent to explore new ways of functioning. Three factors appear to be influential in determining this; whether the children of the family are younger or older, the size of the age gap between own children and fostered adolescent and the period of child rearing in which the foster family is operating.

Whether children of the family are younger or older

Generally speaking there appear to be more hazards and fewer benefits for the adolescent when children of the family are younger than the fostered adolescent. In the research study, it was exceptional to find younger children appreciating adolescent's attempts to help look after them. Hostile or potentially destructive interaction was noted in a number of cases, but appeared not to have been known about by foster parents at the time. The evidence suggests that the tension for foster parents between their wish to protect their own young children from physical harm and their wish to work therapeutically with a difficult adolescent becomes hard to manage at times. Possibly foster parents 'not knowing' and their children 'not telling' them might both be understood as attempts to avoid this dilemma.

'Adult children' still living intermittently at home or locally were sometimes able to provide an entry for an adolescent into their social network. Some may become attachment figures for the adolescent supporting them while they negotiate peer group and work relationships. Their approval or disapproval can become very important to the adolescent.

The age gap between own children and fostered adolescents

In line with earlier and more recent research (Trasler, 1960; Parker, 1966; Kalveston, 1976; Cautley, 1980; Berridge and Cleaver, 1987), the study found that a narrow age gap militated against fostered adolescents experiencing the foster home as a secure base for exploration. This was particularly so when the age gap was less than four years and the children of the family were younger than the adolescent. It appeared that the children often got caught between the parental expectation that they would help and befriend, their own role confusion vis a vis the fostered adolescent and their developmental need to distance themselves from their families and possibly to rebel. The result was interaction characterised by ambiguity and ambivalence. When the child of the family is older than the adolescent, they are more likely to take the initiative to distance themselves, thus decreasing the sense of discomfort for both of them.

The period of child rearing

Families are likely to function differently when their children are at different ages, and this pattern will be superimposed on the patterns of distance regulation characteristic of a particular family throughout its family life cycle. For example, a family with preschool aged children is likely to operate within a smaller circle than is the case when the child starts school and develops friendships with peers and leisure activities. Both child and parents tend to move in widening circles, and both build up experience in negotiating with a widening range of other families and institutions. This means that subsequent children have a different experience of family life than the eldest one.

At the same time as children's explorations take them further afield, both children and parents feel comfortable with increasing distance from each other for longer periods, without knowing precisely where each other is at any point in the day. Shifts in the pattern are likely to occur in line with the growth and development and changing needs of the eldest child in the family.

On this argument, the periods of child rearing were defined by the age of the eldest child at the time a particular adolescent was placed. The early period of child rearing included those families whose eldest child was under 11 years 8 months at the time an adolescent joined the family. The middle period included those whose eldest child was between 11 years 8 months and 17 years 7 months. The late period of child rearing included those whose eldest child was over 17 years 7 months. Matching families at different periods of child rearing with fostered adolescents will be discussed later in this chapter.

Styles of family functioning in relation to adolescents' patterns of attachment and distance regulation

A number of family systems concepts have been identified and discussed in Parts 1 and 2. Here they are expanded and each is discussed in relation to dimensions and styles of family functioning likely to be helpful or unhelpful to adolescents in care functioning in particular ways. A final section is concerned with matching adolescents' patterns of distance regulation with styles of family functioning.

Family's capacity for distance regulation

The concept of distance regulation within family systems was introduced in Chapter 3. Distance regulation concerns the psychosocial distance or closeness people maintain between themselves and significant others, it includes physical, social and emotional components. In Chapter 8 some of the difficulties between adolescents and their foster parents were formulated in terms of the adolescents' restricted capacity for distance regulation between them and their attachment figures. They may be unable to tolerate closeness or be fearful of venturing out alone or they may oscillate to and fro between the extremes of these two poles.

Some families function in close knit, some in over close or

156

enmeshed ways, and others are more distanced. These ideas are already familiar within the literature of family therapy (see for example Minuchin, 1974). It is unlikely that families functioning at one extreme or the other of distancing or enmeshment would be selected for fostering. However, within the broad middle range, it may well be that adolescents with certain patterns of behaviour will fit more comfortably in some families where they are likely to generate less stress than in others.

An adolescent who is anxiously attached may fit comfortably in a close knit family, but would be experienced as stressful in a more distanced family. An adolescent who behaves in an emotionally detached manner is likely to fit comfortably in a more distanced family but be experienced as stressful by a close knit family. A good example of the latter would be the Murphy's experience with Frank Little who had spent most of his life in a large residential special school and whose behaviour was emotionally detached. For the Murphy's, Frank felt like a 'caged animal' in their small house where it seemed as though he was constantly walking into the walls. This got so much under their skin that Mr Murphy, embarking on a repair job in the house to calm his nerves, ended up accidently knocking a hole through the wall.

How might close knit or distanced family functioning be recognised? The initial pen pictures that follow include some of the factors that are more likely to be recognisable during the initial assessment and preparation period. Other factors which are more likely to become apparent once an adolescent is placed with them, are included later in this chapter.

A family that functions in a close knit manner. Family members are likely to spend a good deal of their time together, activities tend to be shared and often parents and children share together in the same sports or other leisure pursuits. Members of a close knit family usually assume that they will know where each family members is at a given point in time and what they are doing. Family members are sensitive to each others moods and feelings. In a close knit family, members' sphere of operation outside the family, for example in relation to their children's schools, may be relatively limited. They may claim to welcome family members' friends into the family but not to be in the habit of visiting other people's houses outside the extended family. Members will tend to attribute feelings, thoughts and attitudes to each other without being aware that they are doing so or checking out the validity of the attribution. When they are together they may tend to speak for each other instead of allowing each member to speak for themselves. This gives a sense of an undifferentiated 'family' approach to a particular issue like appying to foster, in which it is difficult to disentangle the views of individual family members.

A family that functions in a more distanced manner. Family members are likely to spend a higher proportion of their time engaged in separate activities and they may spend a considerable amount of their time outside the family. Meal times may provide almost the sole meeting point for the family as a whole, and even these may be staggered. This often means that the family has to rely on more formal structures for communication such as agreed family rules, including rules that children leave information as to their whereabouts, a notice board, or regular 'family meetings'. Each member of the family is likely to have their own set of friends which may not be known to other family members, particularly as they are more likely to meet their friends outside the family. In families functioning in a very distanced manner, members are likely to experience difficulties in communicating with each other, and may appear to have difficulty in being aware of each others needs and wishes. A sense of unease about this state of affairs may be one of the factors in their wish to foster, for example they may think it would be helpful to their family to provide an adolescent companion for an adolescent member of the family with whom other family members feel out of touch. Family members may give a sense of being a collection of distantly related individuals rather than a family.

It will be clear from these pen pictures that distance regulation may also vary to some degree with the age and stage of development of the children of the family. Not only do children progressively extend their circle of exploration, but parents progressively allow them greater freedom to do so. On this argument we might expect that parents will be geared for greater proximity to young children during the early period of their child rearing. If an adolescent joins their family they are likely to be involved in a sudden change to allow for the more appropriate distance between themselves and the fostered adolescent. Some of the extreme anxieties experienced by the Henderson family when Gina Fitzgerald went missing, which were discussed in chapter 6 might be accounted for in this way.

There is the possibility that an adolescent might fit almost too comfortably into a family in relation to their respective patterns of distance regulation. For example an adolescent's emotionally detached behaviour may go unchallenged in a family who behave in a distanced manner.

Assessing the family's capacity for distance regulation in relation to the needs of particular adolescents. The brief pen pictures in this section provide initial guidelines for assessing families functioning in a more close knit or distanced manner. Most fostered adolescents are likely to do best in families who are able to move easily between intimacy and distance, such families are most able to adapt without excessive discomfort to adolescents' existing patterns of distance regulation and gradually enable them to extend their range. However, provided patterns of close or distanced functioning are not extreme, families may still be able to work effectively with certain adolescents.

Families who function in a more distanced fashion may well be able to accomodate adolescents behaving in emotionally detached ways so that the placement does not disrupt, but they need to avoid collusion with the adolescent's distancing if they are to effect change. The Page's work with Eddie Lewis, described in chapter 6, failed in this respect, and the placement eventually drifted apart when the Pages and their social worker made no effort to contact and work with Eddie when he was in the neighbourhood of the foster home during an episode of going missing. Families whose functioning is close knit may have difficulty tolerating adolescents behaving in an emotionally detached or hostile, ambivalent ways. While such a family may respond with the proximity demanded by an adolescent who behaves in an anxiously attached way, they may have more difficulty encouraging and tolerating exploration, which would be the necessary next step for the adolescent.

The flexibiltiy of the foster family as a system which is joined by a new member

The fact that a family is willing to open its doors to an adolescent does not guarantee its flexibility. The entry of a new member into the family system involves a shift in family equilibrium. The degree of discomfort this causes both adolescent and family will depend on the family's confidence in its stability and its concern for its vulnerability. This dimension influences the degree of protectiveness shown towards the family's own children. It is argued elsewhere (Downes, 1987) that a foster family's concern for its own vulnerability is likely to be greatest when they have young children of their own and particularly in the early period of child rearing.

The foster family obviously needs to be flexible enough to make room for a new member if it is to be effective. When an adolescent joins the family, each family member needs to be able to shift their position to some extent in response to the adolescent, rather than the family prescribing a slot into which the adolescent must fit. In an inflexible family, the shifts in alliances and the repatterning which inevitably take place when a new member joins, will be influenced more by the family's expectations of how the newcomer is going to fit in, than by the needs and characteristics of the adolescent. A quite common example would be when adolescents are expected to act as companions to children of the family or, conversely, not to spend time with them, but to develop new friendship networks of their own. In either form of inflexibility there is a restriction on the adolescent's leeway for first settling in and then extending his/her distance range in developing friendships outside the family.

Discomfort at the arrival of a new member to join the family may be indicated in preoccupations with sameness and differences between fostered adolescent and the rest of the family. An example of sameness would be a mutual insistence from the beginning of the placement that adolescent and children of the family are 'like sisters', this may indicate a rather enmeshed family. Preoccupation with differences may indicate a rather distanced family, an example would be a family that perceives the fostered adolescent as so different from themselves that he cannot be expected to abide by the existing family rules about times for being in for meals or at night or the use of the phone. Preoccupation with sameness or differences are both indicative of a certain lack of flexibility.

Discomfort may also be indicated by a preoccupation with the way information passes or fails to pass across the intergenerational boundary between parents and children. This concern may show itself through a predominant theme of 'telling' on the part of children and adolescents. A fostered adolescent may challenge a child of the family to 'tell' on him when he makes unsanctioned phone calls, this may put the child of the family under a lot of stress as he attempts to maintain a middle position, neither condoning or 'telling', but at the same time feeling alienated from his family and 'pushed out' by the fostered adolescent. Alternatively the theme may be what the foster parents do or do not know is going on in their family. Where foster parents are avoiding or evading an issue, a young child of the family may act as 'symptom bearer' pointing to the discomfort and difficulty in the whole family.

The concepts of family myths and family scripts were introduced in Chapter 3. A family that is unreflective about its family myths, that is the way its members define themselves and approach the world are less likely to show flexibility in their approach to an adolescent joining the family. There will be a greater likelihood of collusion with the adolescent, if the family myths of the two families overlap or conflict between them if they do not. In either case, there is the danger of less reflective space being available to the adolescent.

Assessing the flexibility of the family system in relation to the needs of particular adolescents. A family whose equilibrium is held in close, connected interrelations is likely to be least help to a hostile, ambivalent adolescent who will enter into the closeness, forming potentially disruptive alliances within the family. A close knit family's concern with its own vulnerability may result in premature moves to protect its vulnerable members and exclude the adolescent. Such a family may be more helpful to a self reliant but emotionally detached adolescent, provided the family can tolerate his/her distancing.

A family whose equilibrium is held in distanced, separate interrelationships may be more able to help a hostile, angry adolescent. Such a family may provide a comfortable placement for an emotionally detached adolescent, because of their lesser expectations of intimacy. Here the danger may be that they will collude with the adolescent's distancing, in such a way that the system shifts to an evasive style of functioning, as appeared to happen between Eddie Lewis and the Page family.

The permeability of the boundary between the family and the outside world

This concept was introduced in Chapter 3. The permeability of the family boundary will determine the nature of the transactions across that boundary and the ease whereby family members, other people or information passes to and fro between the family and the world outside. It follows that a permeable boundary to the foster family is an important criterion for effective fostering of adolescents, whatever their particular pattern of behaviour.

If a family has a permeable boundary, its members are likely to be more involved with other systems: school, work, clubs, church, friends and neighbours, and their own extended family. They will be in a position to ease the adolescent's transition to school or work, they are more likely to provide encouragement to him and his birth family to keep in touch with each other and to facilitate his efforts to make new friends in the neighbourhood. When the boundary is permeable, adolescents who go missing are likely to be welcomed back without fuss, or angry exchanges on the threshold in the early hours of the morning, as happened, for example, with Gina Fitzgerald, placed with the Hendersons and described in Chapter 6. The end of the placement will be negotiated with a view to continuity of contact, with the foster family taking their share in the initiative.

A family with an impermeable boundary whose transactions across that boundary are more restricted may tend towards a view of the world outside the family as unfriendly, hostile, or corrupt. One of the dangers in such families is that they develop an agenda for the adolescent which is primarily a protective one, and where exploration and risk taking is not encouraged. The adolescent is warned against allowing himself to be exploited but not actively helped to negotiate the world in which he will shortly be expected to survive, as happened in Ben Little's placement with the Wilkinsons, described in Chapters 5 and 7. During episodes of going missing, such as those which the Hendersons described in Chapter 6 concerning Gina Fitzgerald, families may perceive the adolescent, in her absence, as both victim and destructive saboteur of the foster family. This makes re-entry even more difficult for an adolescent who may also, when absent from her foster home, be perceiving it as rejecting. Another danger is that a family who regard themselves as a bastion against an evil and unfriendly world, or who merely find virtue in 'keeping themselves to themselves' might be over cautious in its involvement in local institutions and activities outside the family.

Assessing the permeability of the family boundary in relation to the needs of particular adolescents. A permeable boundary to the foster family appears an important criterion for successful fostering of adolescents. It will be tested initially in negotiations with social workers and agency during the assessment and preparation period, although it is important to remember how anxious most families feel during this period.

Possibly families with less permeable boundaries may have some success with anxiously attached or passive, emotionally detached adolescents, both of whom may require a longer period in which to experience the security and reliability of the family before they are ready to venture out. At the point they are ready, however, the family would need considerable help if they are to encourage and support the adolescent's explorations.

Family capacity for alliance formation

The process of alliance formation between adolescent and foster parent was first elucidated at the end of chapter 4 and in chapter 8 was considered more generally as an essential parenting skill if an adolescent is to experience a foster parent as providing a secure base from which he or she may negotiate the transition into adult life. In systems terms, an alliance formed between a foster parent and an adolescent would be regarded as the formation of a new subsystem within the family which will affect all existing subsystems. This process may be hindered in a family functioning inflexibly, as the new alliance is more likely to constitute a threat to other existing subsystems involving children of the family and the other adult partner.

163

Alliance formation is likely to be initiated and consolidated by a foster parent giving close and sensitive attention to the adolescent's cues. Empathy is essential if the adolescent is to experience his foster parents as working for him. Empathy has been helpfully redefined within a framework of attachment theory and systems theory as 'the ability to take account of the goals and plans of other people' (Heard, 1978, p. 71). Without a degree of open shared meaning between a foster parent and an adolescent there is little likelihood of an alliance forming. This is one reason why the family's capacity for open, shared emotional communication, an idea introduced in Chapter 3, is of considerable importance.

An enmeshed family, preoccupied with 'sameness' may unwittingly impose their own goals on an adolescent, for example that she adopt their particular version of good manners. A distanced family preoccupied with 'differences' may have equal difficulty taking the adolescents goals and aspirations into account but for different reasons, in that they will assume that the adolescent wishes to function in an entirely different manner to themselves without being sensitive to the extent or ways in which a particular adolescent wishes to feel part of the family.

Attention, empathy and acceptance of the worth and validity of the adolecent's goals leads into joint endeavour on the adolescents behalf. This is likely to be in connection with something he or she very much wants but fears failure. This in turn provides an arena where feedback may be offered, how feedback will be received will depend partly on the adolescent's distorted expectations and perceptions of reality, but also on the foster parents' ability to communicate in a straightforward, open, feeling manner. This was well illustrated in Chapters 4 and 5 in the detailed study of Andy West and Mr Armstrong engaged in job seeking, and in the continued account of Andy's concern over his relationship with his father.

To be effective, feedback needs to be direct, truthful, without exaggeration, evasion or emotional loading. Such feedback has the effect of challenging the adolescent's global views of himself, for example as being wholly dislikeable, out of control, destructive or a totally helpless victim of circumstances. Limit setting within the context of direct and truthful feedback, leaves the responsibility for decisions about action with the adolescent, while making the foster parent's position quite clear.

Sometimes the adolescent's goals may be modified as an outcome of feedback particularly if this takes the form of constructive reframing. This is a variant of the view of the bottle as half empty or half full. It will involve hearing the adolescent's view of himself in relation to others, for example, birth family or employers and offering back a reformulated version which puts a slightly different but not knowingly untruthful construction on events. In Chapter 2 the outcome of Tom Skipper's rediscovery of his vagrant, mentally ill mother was that he started wondering whether there might be a home with her when he left care. After one visit, when Tom was struggling to sort out his mixed feelings for his mother, Mr Armstrong was able to reflect back Tom's simultaneous wish to care for her and his embarrassment at her bizarre behaviour. Following this Tom was able to come to his own decision about his future relations with his mother. The sensitivity of the response lies both in its accuracy and in its timing. At the other end of the spectrum families may engage in destructive reframing, for example over an adolescent's anticipated capacity to cope with life once the placement ends, this is ineffective in influencing goals and does nothing to help adolescents take responsibility for their lives.

A foster family's capacity for constructive reframing is likely to vary with the permeability of the family boundary, bearing in mind the frequent connection between impermeable boundaries and a mistrustful stance toward the world outside the family. This is another way of saying that the nature and quality of the relationship develops out of the meanings attributed by the participants to the interaction. Where a constructive meaning is attributed to events and interactions this is likely to be followed by constructive reframing to the adolescent and the process spirals in a helpful direction. But equally, the opposite process may be set in motion, which if not checked usually leads to a disrupted placement.

Assessing the family's capacity for alliance formation in relation to the needs of particular adolescents. The capacity for flexible reforming of subsystems within the family would seem essential for successful alliance formation between foster parent and adolescent. It is through such an alliance that the adolescent experiences the foster family as a secure base, and is able to move out across the family boundary to engage in age appropriate psychosocial tasks.

Alliance formation usually presents fewest difficulties for foster parents caring for anxiously attached adolescents. An ability to listen, especially to underlying levels in the adolescent's cues may be partially assessed ahead of placement by assessing family members ability to listen to each other. The same is true of the family's ability to communicate with each other openly and with feeling. Offering feedback and constructive reframing may be learned with experience, provided the initial capacity for attention and empathy is present.

With angry, ambivalent adolescents the cues may be more difficult to hear and interpret. For example, Mrs Henderson heard but did not understand the anxiety underlying Gina Fitzgerald's insolence to her headmistress. Feedback involves a considerable amount of spelling out of consequences of behaviour and limit setting if responsibility for actions is to remain with the adolescent, and foster parents avoid being sucked into their powerful destructive dynamic.

Alliance formation is most difficult with emotionally detached adolescents who provide few cues and may shun or fear feedback. An alliance with a foster parent may be providing a secure base for an emotionally detached adolescent, long before they are able to convey this experience back to their foster parents. The danger is that foster parents give up, feeling that they are not helping, because the adolescent has been unable to provide them with any positive feedback. Social workers have a vital part to play in 'constructive reformulation' of the alliance to foster parents, to reassure them that they are valued by the adolescent against all the apparent evidence.

Family's ability to establish a safe transitional zone

The concept of the safe transitional zone was introduced in Chapter 3. A foster family provides a safe transitional zone for an adolescent through a member of the family moving out with the adolescent into a situation in which he or she might otherwise

166

have been overwhelmed by anxiety and unable to function effectively. This provision may be planned or fortuitous, as was illustrated in Chapter 4 when Mr Armstrong moved with Andy West through his negotiations with the careers officer and prospective employers during his search for work. The safe transitional zone operates through an existing alliance between the adolescent and a family member or a new one formed for a particular purpose. In a sense the family boundary temporarily extends outwards into the wider social system, such that the adolescent's secure base is on hand while he is very anxious and unsure of himself.

Not every movement out of the foster family with an adolescent on the part of a foster parent can be regarded as creating a safe transitional zone. This will depend on whether or not an alliance between adolescent and foster parent has been established. It is doubtful, for example, that when in Chapter 4, Mrs Henderson accompanied Gina Fitzgerald to an interview with her headmistress, that this was experienced by Gina as providing her with a safe transitional zone, as the alliance was not with Gina but between Mrs Henderson and the headmistress. Nor, in Chapter 7 would the Goldman's insistence that Kevin Flynn accompany them on outings rather than remain alone in the foster home, create a safe transitional zone for Kevin, as this arrangement answered the Goldman's anxieties rather than Kevin's. This example provides an illustration of a close knit family who were too frightened of the stranger in their midst to be able to form an alliance with him.

Assessing the family's capacity for creating a safe transitional zone in relation to the needs of particular adolescents. The capacity of a foster family to form a safe transitional zone for an adolescent, for a particular purpose, is related to the permeability of the family boundary and family members' capacity to form an alliance with the adolescent. This is because the foster parent neeeds to feel at ease moving out with the adolescent into an uncertain and possibly frustrating situation.

Provision of a safe transitional zone may also be affected by the period of child rearing the family have reached. In the early period of child rearing the family may have had less opportunity to extent itself into the community and its own explorations may well be confined to a smaller circle nearer home. As their own children grow older and move further afield, so the family are likely to extend their field of operations and some of the territory in which the adolescent is likely to operate grows familiar to them.

As with alliance formation, safe transitional zones are more readily useable by anxiously attached adolescents or hostile ambivalent adolescents. They are likely to be used less readily by emotionally detached adolescents.

Family's capacity for collaborative working and establishing a coffer dam

This concept was introduced at the end of Chapter 3 and was illustrated in Chapter 4. It is a useful analogy for describing other coalitions that foster parents may need to establish while at the same time maintaining a strong alliance with the adolescent. In contrast with a safe transitional zone which is concerned with a two way alliance between foster parent and adolescent operating outside the usual family boundary, this is concerned with three way working or working as part of a network of professional helpers.

In contrast to a safe transitional zone which is formed out of a subsystem of the family, a coffer dam is a new system set up for a particular purpose concerning the adolescent and it is likely to operate with its own set of subsystems. Examples of coffer dams would include collaborative working arrangements involving a foster parent, adolescent and any combination of birth family members, social worker, employer, adolescent's friends, etc. which operates in such a way that it enables an adolescent's anxiety, hostility or ambivalence to be contained without disastrous acting out or splitting. In order to do this, the adolescent's needs, wishes and anxieties and the perceptions, views and feelings of other members forming the coffer dam, need to be held in tension. Coffer dams tend to fail when coalitions between some members are strong and other members are weak.

Assessing the family's capacity for establishing and working within a coffer dam in relation to the needs of particular adolescents. As with the formation of safe transitional zones, the foster family's capacity for establishing coffer dams will be partially dependent on the permeability of the family boundary. It will also depend on family members' skill in forming an alliance with the adolescent, as this needs either to precede or not challenge coalitions between foster parents and other adults outside the family. It will further depend on the foster parents ability to work well with other adults within the adolescent's network.

The capacity to form a coffer dam is important in work with all adolescents, it seems particularly difficult with passive, emotionally detached and hostile, ambivalent adolescents.

Matching adolescents' patterns of distance regulation with style of family functioning

The following summary provides guidelines for matching adolescents showing a particular pattern of disturbed behaviour or distance regulation with families with a particular style of functioning.

Adolescents showing a pattern of anxious attachment, or the need for close proximity to foster family members

They may feel comfortable in a close knit family, which may be likely to have a less permeable boundary. Conversely their presence and demands may create more stress in a family who function in a more distanced manner.

The difficulty for the close knit family may come at the point that the adolescent begins to experience them as a secure base, and needs encouragement to explore outside the family boundary. In their favour would be the anxiously attached adolescent's capacity for forming alliances and making use of a safe transitional zone or coffer dam. The family, particularly if it is engaged in the early stages of child rearing, may need support in its negotiations with other adults in the adolescent's network

Adolescents showing a pattern of hostile, ambivalent behaviour, who veer rapidly between closeness and distance

These adolescents are unlikely to do well in a close knit family or one concerned with its own vulnerability. Probably families

169

engaged in the early stages of child rearing are best avoided for this reason. They may do well in a more disengaged family with a permeable family boundary, allowing for easy passage to and fro. Family members will need to pick up on the adolescent's distorted cues, when seeking proximity, given that they do this, adolescents behaving in hostile, ambivalent ways are able to form alliances and make use of safe transitional zones. Foster parents need to be able to collaborate with other adults involved with the adolescent so that the adolescents conflicting perceptions and goals may be contained. This provides adolescents with an opportunity to shift from acting out behaviour with the potential for splitting the caregiving network, to more reflective reappraisal of their own behaviour and relationships.

Adolescents showing a pattern of emotionally detached behaviour or the need to distance themselves from foster family members

They are more likely to feel comfortable in a family who function in a more distanced manner themselves. The danger is that a collusive, evasive pattern of interaction develops if explicit, agreed agenda is not kept to the fore. Family members need particularly well developed skills in alliance formation, as these adolescents have little capacity for this themselves. Once an alliance has been formed, they can make good use of safe transitional zones and a coffer dam form of collaboration may help to lessen the likelihood of such adolescents taking flight to and fro between carers to avoid closeness.

Adolescents showing a more self reliant form of emotionally detached behaviour may also be able to function from the base of a close knit family, provided the family is sufficiently confident to allow the adolescent considerable rein to stake out his or her preferred distance first. From this distance, an adolescent may negotiate, moving closer at their own pace.

10 Constructing a secure base for the caregiving network: the role of the social worker

Chapter 8, focussed on the processes of interaction between adolescent and foster parent, and also outlined the skills which a foster parent needs to exercise if he or she is to be experienced by an adolescent as a secure base from which to negotiate the transition to adult life. In Chapter 9 the systemic functioning of the foster family as a secure base for its own members and for the adolescent was the focus, and ways were considered in which foster families with different styles of functioning might work with adolescents with differing patterns of attachment. This chapter extends the focus so that the adolescent and foster family is considered within the context of the whole caregiving network. It is concerned with how the caregiving network might operate as a secure base for the adolescent and with some of the difficulties that commonly arise. It focuses particularly on a crucial social work role if this network is to function effectively in the best interests of the adolescent.

As well as the foster family, the adolescent's caregiving network usually consists of members of their birth family, other previous attachment figures such as residential social workers, and the adolescent's social worker. It may also include other helping professionals such as a psychiatrist or clinical psychologist, teachers or, occasionally, an employer. Social services managers are also likely to be involved in case conferences and reviews

171

where the adolescent's placement is reviewed and where major decisions concerning the adolescent are made.

It will be argued that as with the foster family, it is useful to consider the systemic functioning of the caregiving network as it is influenced by the adolescent's behaviour and in turn is influential. When its members work together flexibly, openly, non-exclusively and without rivalry it has the potential for being experienced as a secure base for the adolescent. Conversely, when there are difficulties in the way the network functions as a system or in its subsystems, the adolescent is likely to feel less safe, and less able to make good use of the placement.

The research study and this book has focussed on the interaction between adolescent and foster family members and has considered foster parents as the direct workers with the adolescent. This has left open the question of the social worker's role: is it appropriate for a social worker or other practitioners to be doing direct work with adolescents while they are placed with foster parents, alternatively, is the social worker's role to be confined to fulfilling minimum statutory requirements or case management?

Experience from the study and from practice indicates that placements are most effective and mutually satisfying for all concerned when foster parents, social workers and other practitioners are able to take a flexible approach to their work, depending on the needs and wishes of the adolescent and the aptitudes and skills of members of the caregiving network. Sometimes the adolescent's social worker will be engaged in direct work with the adolescent around a particular issue, sometimes a foster parent will be working in a similar way, at other times a practitioner from another discipline, such as a psychiatrist, psychologist or teacher will be working with the adolescent. Flexible arrangements are possible when all concerned are able to avoid rivalry with each other and with an adolescent's birth parents to become 'better parents' to the adolescent.

This chapter is not concerned with direct work with the adolescent. The principles and practice of direct work with adolescents undertaken by foster parents have already been discussed and can be adapted for use by social workers and other practitioners. While the statutory duties of social services departments and social workers will be borne in mind, they are not the focus of this book and are well described in Volume 3 of *The*

Children Act: Guidance and Regulations (Department of Health, 1991). Rather, the chapter focusses on a different role for the social worker, a role which is likely to be vital if the placement is to be effective; that of working at one remove, or more than one remove from the adolescent.

Foster parents and other members of the caregiving network, like adolescents, need the experience of a secure base if they are to work well together and they will particularly need someone to provide this if they are having difficulties in this respect. The chapter discusses ways in which social workers may enable members of the foster family and others within the caregiving network to work together with the adolescent and with each other. Provided members of the network are able to feel confident and safe enough with each other, they are likely to be able to work reflectively together and to bear a good deal of each other's uncertainty and risk taking in the course of a placement. In other words, members will be acting as a secure base for each other. The social worker's task is to help them to construct this secure base.

The difficulties that arise in caregiving networks are legion. Some have been well illustrated in Part 2 and only require a brief reference here, many others have not been considered at all. Issues arising in four different subsystems of the caregiving network have been selected by way of example, those concerning difficulties that have not been illustrated or discussed elsewhere in the book are given a fuller treatment. Work with the adolescent's birth family is only touched on as it is impossible to do justice to it here.

The selection of these particular subsystems and issues was partly determined by the scope of the original research data. As the research did not focus directly on the social worker's role or seek accounts of their work from the social workers concerned with these placements, the accounts of what social workers did and the suggestions as to how it would be helpful for them to operate come from other sources. These include reports during the course of the research by adolescents and foster parents of what social workers did and what they found helpful or unhelpful, records made by the researcher about the way adolescents and foster parents made use of her in the course of the research interviews, and practice experience.

In practice, social workers move between subsystems of the

caregiving network and sometimes operate on the interface between them, encompassing a wide range of tasks undertaken in relation to a young person being looked after by the local authority, quite apart from the direct work with the young person concerned. These tasks require at least two workers for each placement, one whose main responsibility is the adolescent, and the other who will work with the foster family and other members of the caregiving network. In some instances a third worker working with the adolescent's parents may be appropriate, but this is outside the scope of this book. One aim of this chapter is to outline a framework for these tasks, perhaps no more than a preliminary sketch, so that they can begin to be understood as part of a coherent plan of work and so that their crucial importance for the outcome of placements is appreciated.

Work with the following four subsystems of the caregiving network have been selected:

1. Working with foster parents.
2. Facilitating the alliance between adolescents and their foster parents.
3. Working with the whole foster family, including the foster parents' children.
4. Working with the caregiving network which includes other professionals and may include members of the adolescent's birth family.

Working with foster parents

Helping angry foster parents to maintain objectivity

Adolescent's unresolved feelings about previous relationships and their consequent misperceptions often make it difficult for foster parents to maintain objectivity. Donald Winnicott describes a time when he and his wife fostered a disturbed 9 year old boy. He is not specific about the boy's awful behaviour that engendered hate in him. He describes what he did about it; at crises, he would take him, by bodily strength, and put him outside the front door, where there was a bell for the boy to ring when he was ready to be readmitted.

Mrs Henderson's description in Chapter 6 of the fury that she and her husband experienced when the police returned Gina Fitzgerald to them at 3.30am has a similar ring of truth, but also serves to emphasise the differences between managing a 9 year old and a hefty adolescent! However, Winnicott makes a number of points which are also applicable to work with adolescents. First that foster parents need to be sufficiently self aware to be able to separate what he calls their 'objective' reaction to bad behaviour from reactions arising from their own earlier experiences; Winnicott points out that good supervision or consultation is essential to gain the necessary reflective space for this. Secondly, that only 'objective' reactions should be expressed. Thirdly, that if the foster parent does not express his reaction then and there, the situation is likely to escalate, and fourthly, that this may well be the only genuine feeling that can reach the young person at that moment, and as such is of great value to him or her. Commenting on his words of 'objective hate' to his 9 year old foster son, Winnicott says:

> I think these words were important from the point of view of his progress, but they were mainly important in enabling me to tolerate the situation without not letting out, without losing my temper and without every now and again murdering him. (Winnicott, 1958, p. 200)

Foster parents sometimes become so overwhelmed by the strength of their anger that it is not easy for them to tell adolescents 'objectively' that they hate a particular aspect of their behaviour or to point out how destructive they are being.

The social worker's task. It is easy to criticise foster parents' negative attitudes when one is not in the front line, but it is much more difficult for people to manage negative feelings when they are in the position of direct carer. The social worker needs first to offer foster parents their full attention and encouragement to explore and express what they really feel, without fear of criticism or without the social worker immediately turning the focus away from them back to the adolescent with possible explanations for his or her bad behaviour. For this reason alone, this is not usually a job that it is appropriate for the adolescent's social worker to take on, as a worker in that role will inevitably be primarily concerned about what is happening to the adolescent, and will find it difficult to stay with foster parents' negative feelings for long enough and to remain nonjudgemental.

The aim is to enable an angry foster parent to eventually be able to recover a more reflective stance. An indication that this point has been reached is that they are able to begin to think the incident through from the stance of the adolescent, and to think about the impact each has had on the other. At this point, but not before, a discussion may be helpful on possible ways of intervening or responding in the event of another episode of escalating anger.

Working with foster parents who are operating on a hidden agenda

This section discusses situations where attitudes and feelings are covert, and are sometimes not fully recognised by foster parents themselves. In the course of the research interviews with foster families, foster parents and adolescents sometimes interjected comments which indicated how they saw the purpose of the placement, what it was they were aiming to do and how they evaluated the outcome of the placement. Inevitably, the purposes or agenda set by foster parents were not always in line with the aspirations of a particular adolescent and this was particularly the case in relation to adolescent's agenda in relation to their birth family and their plans for reaching this position. For example, in nine placements foster parents implied that they wished to discourage an adolescent's links with their birth family. They might seek to do this either by a policy of non-collaboration with people significant to the adolescent, or by discouraging the adolescent's contact with these people.

Foster parents would also sometimes formulate the purpose of the placement in terms of winning adolescents' commitment to the foster family's ways of thinking and behaving, rather than encouraging them to formulate their own approach to life and life style. Sometimes this would be expressed as a wish that the adolescent would make a clean break with his or her birth family and perhaps eventually set up home somewhere near the foster parents. The motivation for this approach often lay in foster parents' anxiety about what could realistically be achieved in a

176

time limited placement and the sense that they needed much longer for any lasting changes to be consolidated.

Sometimes it was possible for foster parents to be explicit about their views and to enter into open debate with adolescents, for example over the relative merits of returning to their home area or creating their new home base near to the foster parents. When this happened, adolescent and foster parent could usually agree to differ. However in seven out of the eleven placements studied prospectively, foster parents agenda was seen to contain major 'hidden' elements. That is, elements that were not stated explicitly to the adolescent, or indeed to the social worker. Often this aspect of the dynamic between foster parent and adolescent became much clearer once the placement had ended and foster parents and adolescent were separately reviewing, with the researcher, what had happened over the course of the placement.

In each case the foster parents' hidden agenda became a major issue in the interaction between them and the adolescent. It seemed as though what could not be made explicit would be acted out in the interaction. For example when Clare Dobson declared herself pregnant her foster parents inwardly resolved that she must leave within three months because they believed that if she remained in the foster home it would have an adverse effect on their two younger children. They were unable to share this plan with the Clare, or to re-examine their presupposition. Meanwhile Clare's disorganised, disruptive behaviour became increasingly extreme, bringing the placement to an end even sooner than her foster parents had intended. Ben's foster parents privately hoped to direct him away from his plans to live with his older brothers, fearing that they would exploit and corrupt him, and discourage him from working. Ben held firmly to his plan but experienced such incapacitating anxiety over the ending of the placement that he lost his job. The evidence points towards inexplicit or hidden agenda constituting a powerful and unhelpful dynamic in a placement.

The social worker's task. The skill lies in identifying and finding ways of enabling foster parents to share with the adolescent and the social worker those aspects of their agenda which they fear may not please them. While foster parents may be concerned to protect the adolescent from harm, and their own family from damage, they may also wish to avoid confrontation and conflict at the price of foregoing open communication with the adolescent. If the social worker can enable them to examine their 'worst fears' about what might happen if they were more open with the adolescent, some of these fears may, on re-examination, appear to be realistic and some unrealistic, but they will be less global.

This will only happen if foster parents feel safe. It is essential that this exploration takes place without foster parents feeling that such sharing of judgemental attitudes or irrational fears will be used against them. An acceptance of angry feelings and harsh judgements as common to all, including the social worker, may be effective in enabling foster parents to get back in touch with the adolescent's needs and the meaning of his or her behaviour.

When foster parents are exploring attitudes and fears that they have so far been unable to communicate openly to the adolescent, they are likely to need to do this on their own or as a couple, with the worker. The next stage may involve the worker in a session with the foster parents and adolescent where the worker's task is to provide a safe base for more open communication to be risked. This aspect of work at one remove will be explored in the next section.

Affirming to foster parents their value to the adolescent

Carey and Stein (1984) in their consumer study of young people leaving care conclude:

> The most important and enduring aspect of the whole experience of care appears to be the ability to find at least one person who is warm, welcoming, tolerant, understanding and always willing to listen (Carey and Stein, 1984, Appendix, p. 6).

It is critical, therefore, that foster parents should understand their importance to adolescents who have been placed. They may need to be convinced of this against the apparent evidence. It was found in the study that more foster parents than adolescents deemed the placement a failure. At the end of placements foster parents often said that they felt they had been of little help to the adolescent, and perhaps someone else might have done better than them. In contrast, an adolescent who had been placed with them would be warm in their appreciation and evaluation of their foster parents.

The social worker's task. Both emotionally detached and angry adolescents are unlikely to reassure their foster parents of their value. The disparagement of the emotionally detached and the hostility of the angry adolescent can be powerfully undermining to foster parents, precipitating disruption of placements and inhibiting contact once a placement ends. Social workers have a vital role to play in 'constructive reformulation' to foster parents of the relationship between them and the adolescent they are caring for. It is usually much more possible at one remove to identify the evidence in the adolescent's behaviour that indicates that their foster parents are valued, even though an adolescent may make great efforts to disguise this from their foster parent and even from themselves.

Facilitating the alliance between adolescents and their foster parents

Alliances develop between adolescents and foster parents to a large extent through what they do together in connection with significant events for the adolescent. In order to support this, there may need to be some reallocation of roles between social workers and foster parents so that foster parents take responsibility for the negotiations with schools, employers, collaboration with the adolescent's birth family, retrieving adolescents who go missing and helping with practical arrangements over the end of the placement.

Helping adolescent and foster family stay in touch with each other after to placement ends

The chapter on 'Aftercare: advice and assistance' in Volume 3 of *The Children Act 1989 Guidance and Regulations* encourages foster families to take a continued interest in young people once they have left their placement, within the provision of the Act which lays upon local authorities a duty to advise and befriend adolescents and young adults who leave care at 16 years or older. This duty remains until the young person is 21 years of age, and is subject to them asking for such help and the local authority considering that they need it. The principles underlying preparation for leaving care recognise that:

> Services for young people must take account of the lengthy process of transition from childhood to adulthood, to reflect the gradual transition of a young person from dependence to independence. The support provided should be, broadly, the support that a good parent might be expected to give (Department of Health, 1991, p. 91).

From the detailed study of Tom Skipper and the examples in Chapter 7 of adolescents leaving their placements it should be clear that even when a great deal of thought and preparation has gone into leaving care and the ending of the placement, the move out may be experienced as traumatic by an adolescent who has experienced previous major disruptions. The net result is that both adolescent and foster parents can be left feeling shaken, rejected or devalued; neither is certain that they will be welcome if they take the initiative to get in touch. The young person may feel that he or she should be able to manage on their own and that they have had their share of care and should give way to others still in care. Foster parents may feel that to make the first move might be to give in to their own anxieties about how their adolescent will cope or their wish to overprotect and that they may be intrusive rather than serving the adolescent's needs.

The social worker's task. Attachment theory normalises our continuing need, throughout life, for reliable people to be available to us. This supports the role of the social worker as aiming to maximise the likelihood of the alliance between foster parents and adolescent surviving the end of the placement. At a practical level the social worker might enable foster parents to take a much greater part in organising the move out than they have done in the past, backed by the agency's resources and consultation. If foster parents help with the arrangements over the end of the placement then their continuity of care and concern is demonstrated, and adolescents are less likely to perceive the foster family boundary

180

hardening impenetrably behind them. The social worker may need to actively encourage meetings between adolescents and foster parents immediately after the move, and help adolescents over their reluctance to invite their ex foster parents to their flat or back home, for fear it will be thought 'not good enough'.

Such policies and practices have financial implications; foster parents will only be able to work in this way if they are supported financially and have sufficient space between placements to give the adolescent who has recently left them the attention he or she is likely to need around the transition out of the placement.

Working with the whole foster family, including foster parents' own children

In Chapter 9 some aspects of the dynamic interaction between children of the family, fostered adolescents and their foster parents were outlined as a focus for assessment. Here some of the characteristic difficulties are reviewed and ways of helping foster families who may be particularly vulnerable in their combined role as foster family and family with their own children are discussed.

Foster parents of young children often appear to be caught in a dilemma between their wish to protect their own young children from physical harm and their wish to work therapeutically with a difficult adolescent. Foster parents 'not knowing' about hostile, sexually abusive or potentially destructive behaviour by fostered adolescents towards their own children who, in turn, fail to tell their parents what is happening, might be understood as attempts to avoid this dilemma.

In a research interview with a foster family after the 16 year old boy they had fostered had gone missing and not returned, Jane, aged 7 years, describes how Paul, aged 16 years, had bullied her:

Jane   Paul was going to hit me with the hammer.
Mr Harding   In fact, he did have a hammer, didn't he?
Jane   Yes, he had one of yours.
Mr Harding   I didn't know anything about this, she never told me, it all happened while I was out at work.

Not only had Jane been unable to tell her parents what had happened, she had also been unable to express her anger to her father for his lack of protection. It seemed likely that her older brother and sister had known of this incident but had colluded in not telling. Paul had a highly emotionally detached pattern of attachment. Here the family appeared to be operating in a similarly disengaged manner, and the placement simply 'faded out' when Paul failed to return. A similar dynamic was discussed in Chapter 6, in relation to Eddie Lewis's placement.

A narrow age gap between fostered adolescent and children of the family militates against fostered adolescents experiencing the foster home as a secure base for exploration. Mutual discomfort is often conveyed through ambiguous and ambivalent communication. This was particularly found to be so in the study when the age gap was less than four years and the children of the family were younger than the adolescent. It appeared that the children often got caught between the parental expectation that they would help and befriend, their own role confusion vis a vis the fostered adolescent and their developmental need to stand back and reappraise their families, which may include some stringent criticisms of the way their parents are responding to the fostered adolescent.

When the child of the family is older than the fostered adolescent, they are more likely to take the initiative to distance themselves, thus decreasing the sense of discomfort for both of them. Jane's 17 year old sister expressed her uncertainty about her own position and role in the family in relation to Paul who was a few months younger than she was:

> we seem to be giving the impression that we weren't in on it, that we sort of...that half the family were involved, but in fact we knew about it although we didn't actually...we weren't actually part of the discussion...We weren't in the dark, which I think is important because...o.k. Mum and Dad are foster parents but the whole family's involved and I think it would be dangerous if we were kept in the dark about things. You know, you might find resentments would grow. Or say your Mum might do

something and we might think it's unfair and if she doesn't say things about what she's going to do or how things were going, it could quite easily happen.

Adult children still living at home or locally are sometimes able to provide an entry for an adolescent into their social network. Some may become attachment figures for the adolescent, supporting them while they negotiate peer group and work relationships. Their approval or disapproval can become very important to the adolescent. This can work well if they understand their significance for the adolescent and their role is acknowledged and valued by their parents. Alternatively it can lead to tensions if foster parents and their adult children become rival 'parents', or the adult child suddenly drops the fostered adolescent for somebody else.

At a joint interview with Harry, aged 21 years, his parents and Tim, aged 18 years, who was fostered by them, Harry had been describing his role as buffer, trouble-shooter and provider of feedback to Tim as he started to test out how to relate socially within Harry's peer group. It was clear that Harry had become a significant attachment figure for Tim. At the end of the interview Tim described the impact it had on him when Jim, another fostered adolescent previously known to Harry, arrived at the foster home. Tim's relationship with Harry seems to have been of greater significance to him than it was to Harry.

> Well, you see, I used to go around with Harry to pubs and that, and I used to get ever so mad because Harry knows Jim from when he was thirteen and lived down that way. And Harry closed his eyes to me, if you see what I mean, and went round with Jim for a bit. I just sort of got fed up and didn't like Jim very much at that time because he sort of stole Harry off me and I didn't know anyone around there at the time and I just felt disowned.

Harry appears to have been unaware of the impact of his behaviour on Tim at the time. Tim subsequently commented that he had been surprised at this first research interview to discover that Harry thought as much of him.

Assuming that foster parents have been alerted during the assessment and preparation period to the difficulties they may need to anticipate between their own children and fostered adolescents, it should not be too difficult for a social worker to encourage foster parents to explore some of these issues. Some issues may be discussed with the foster parent or couple alone, other issues, particularly those concerning blocked communication, may be tackled in whole family sessions.

The social worker's task with a foster parent or foster parent couple. A worker may encourage foster parents to think through how best to explain to their children the job they have taken on. One cannot assume that children will understand or share the same enthusiasm, or necessarily wish to be heavily involved. While this will certainly need to be one of the tasks during the initial preparation period, the issues often need to be thought out afresh before and during each new placement. In the example above, Paul was not the first adolescent this family had fostered.

If foster parents are experiencing a conflict between their wish to foster and their wish to protect their own children, it will be important that they are encouraged to identify this and explore with the worker whether or not there are ways through it. If home is being experienced by their own children as a dangerous place because of the behaviour of a fostered adolescent, then their children's attachment behaviour will be aroused. In some instances, like the example of Jane Harding, it seemed difficult for foster parents to acknowledge their own or their children's anxieties, leaving Jane's parents defensively not knowing what was happening between their children and Paul. By offering the foster parents a secure base, a social worker might first enable them to get back in touch with what is happening. From there they may be able to respond to their own children's needs for protection as well as the adolescent's needs and to find some way through their dilemma. If their anxiety remains high with a range of adolescents, it may be that this is not the best period of their own child rearing for them to be fostering adolescents, and it will be better if they take a decision to stop undertaking this type of fostering between placements rather than in mid-placement.

The social worker's task with the whole family. Work with all members of the family, including young children raises the dilemma of how to hold the balance between involving own children and breaching boundaries of confidentiality concerning the fostered adolescent. Videos made by adolescents about themselves, viewed and discussed by the whole family, might provide a way through this dilemma.

The research interviews constituted an opportunity for the whole family including the fostered adolescent to be together with an outsider for a limited amount of time known in advance to all present with the purpose of focussing on what was happening within the placement. It was striking how often family members used these interviews to say things to each other that they had not thought to say or risked saying before. They frequently commented on how helpful this had been for them. The role of the researcher had been to ask very simple, straightforward questions about what had happened since her last visit and what had changed. She tried to ensure that every one had a chance to contribute, and to pay careful attention to what was said.

Where communication has become blocked between children of the family and fostered adolescents or between children and their parents about fostered adolescents, more skilled work with the whole family will be needed. The aim will be for the worker to present him or herself to the family in such a way that the family as a whole are able to experience him or her as a secure base.

This way of working with families, from a perspective of attachment theory, has been well illustrated by John Byng-Hall (1989). Here the principles of the work are reviewed briefly and applied to the social worker's task with foster families. As a family therapist, Byng-Hall considers that the fundamental aim is to;

> create a secure enough base within therapy for the family to explore how each member, and the family as a unit can provide a secure enough base for each other outside of therapy (Byng-Hall, 1989, p. 228).

He argues that for a family to be able to do this, each family member needs to experience at least one secure attachment and be willing to facilitate or tolerate other members' secure attachments.

In work with foster families where the fostered adolescent may be operating with a very different and more insecure pattern of attachment as compared to those of other family members, the worker's aim remains the same. Often the focus may be on the shift in dynamics that has occured since the adolescent joined the family. Byng-Hall identifies a number of problems arising from insecurities in one relationship spoiling the security of another relationship; these include turning to inappropriate attachment figures, competition for an attachment figure, defensive responses to attachment cues and anticipation that losses similar to those that have happened in the past will recur.

In the Harding family who fostered Paul, it seemed probable that each of these problems were present to some degree. Jane appeared to be turning to her brother and sister rather than to her parents when she was bullied by Paul. Possibly all three children were experiencing their parents as less available to them as attachment figures since Paul had arrived and was causing them all considerable worry. Paul appeared to be in angry competition with Jane, the youngest child of the family for the attention of Mrs Harding. Mr Harding appeared defensively unwilling, perhaps even unable to know what was happening, and was increasingly staying out of the way. Mr and Mrs Harding, who had experienced major losses themselves, appeared to be finding it particularly difficult to confront Paul's increasingly emotionally detached behaviour, for fear of losing him, which is what happened.

Whole family sessions, including the adolescent, need to be built into the support offered to all foster placements at regular but maybe infrequent intervals. This is one form of intervention which will help to construct a secure base for the whole foster family. If the whole family only meet with the worker when crises arise, then the tendency will be to focus on the adolescent's difficult behaviour rather than the family dynamics. Offered on a regular basis as part of the service, the family would be less likely to associate whole family sessions with a sense of failure as a foster family, or to feel that they were being 'pathologised'. They would have more confidence to explore their own family functioning without feeling too defensive about it.

While the placement with the Hardings was underway, the worker, working along the lines suggested by Byng-Hall would first aim to engage every one in the family, including the fostered adolescent, in such a way that they have a sense that their dilemmas are appreciated. This would model non-excluding caregiving. Having gently taken control, and sensing that everyone in the room is anxious about the way the placement is going, it would be wise to quickly address what are their worst fears, giving every one a chance to talk about these.

Everyones contribution is likely to be further valued if the worker can positively reframe disturbed behaviour in terms of its function. It might be suggested that Paul who is from a large family himself may be finding it hard to believe that Mr and Mrs Harding have enough time for him as well as for their own children and this may be why he is fighting Jane over them. Byng-Hall comments:

> In my experience, this form of positive connotation can be one of the most effective ways of introducing a sense of mutual forgiveness. It gives a benign and understandable picture of each other's working models (Byng-Hall, 1990, p. 234)

During the session the worker may change the space between people as a means to changing the nature of the relationship. Mr and Mrs Harding might be asked to sit together to discuss how they could best demonstrate that they have time and space for all four children. Tasks between sessions might include Jane and her father doing something special together each week, and similarly, Paul and his foster mother. Care would need to be taken that Jane's older brother and sister also felt included in the plan, and that Mr and Mrs Harding were given time on their own together.

Working with members of the wider the caregiving network

Meetings of the whole caregiving network including professionals from several disciplines and members of the adolescent's birth family, are built into the course of a placement, either in the form of regular statutory review meetings or as part of a process of decision making at certain critical points in the placement. Sometimes such meetings are called when it becomes clear that different members of this network disagree with one another about what should happen during a placement or after it has ended. Woodhouse and Pengelly, (1991) provide a detailed examination of the dynamics of collaborative work; workers already involved with the placement will find such understanding helpful if they are to avoid getting caught up in defensive manoeuvres which frequently serve to trigger the adolescent's disturbed behaviour still further, leading to unreflective, often panic decisions on the part of professionals which may be regretted subsequently. In complex cases there will be great value in meetings being chaired by someone who is able to hold an independent position, while at the same time struggling to make sense of the dynamics that are being played out.

Here the focus is not on the dynamics of the caregiving network meeting as a whole group, but on a range of difficulties that commonly arise within subsystems of the network.

Working with difficulties within subsystems of the caregiving network

Throughout this study, the focus has been on the alliance that needs to develop between adolescent and foster parent. As long as this is well developed and secure, the adolescent is less likely to experience serious difficulties within the caregiving network as the adolescent will feel well supported in their part in any planning or decision making and foster parents will be confident in the value of what they are doing and will be less likely to get into a position of rivalry with birth parents or other professional workers.

In chapter 9 Robin Skynner's analogy of the coffer dam was used to describe the way in which the caregiving network could itself provide another form of secure base for the adolescent. Operating in this way, members of the caregiving network offer opportunities for joint reflective exploration of the various dilemmas and conflicts facing the adolescent. When its operations are in concert, with no one feeling excluded, the network is more likely to be able to contain the adolescent's anxiety, ambivalence or anger and disastrous acting out or splitting were avoided. Care giving networks are likely to fail to function effectively when there are particular configurations within them involving some coalitions between members being strong, leaving other members feeling excluded and vulnerable. Three common patterns involving weak links in the network are described below.

Strong coalition between foster parent and third party; weak alliance between foster parent and adolescent; weak coalition or conflict between adolescent and third party. An example would be Gina Fitzgerald's insolent reaction in the face of the developing coalition between the headmistress and Mrs Henderson when she went for an interview to a school that had known her previously. This was described in Chapter 4. While Mrs Henderson had doubtless intended to support Gina at this interview, their relationship up to that point had been idealised on both sides, and the ground work for alliance building had not really started. When Gina responded sharply to an apparently innocent question from the headmistress, Mrs Henderson saw her in a new light, as insolent, and failed to respond to Gina's underlying panic. Instead she became increasingly identified with the headmistress's negative view of Gina, and by the end of the meeting there was a strong coalition between foster mother and headmistress which had excluded Gina. Gina never really joined the school and managed to conceal her truancy from her foster mother until it was too late to take remedial action. This pattern tends to happen with emotionally detached adolescents, where everyone has difficulty forming an alliance with them.

The social worker's task. With hindsight, this difficulty might have been overcome if Gina's lack of a well based alliance and the likelihood of her extreme anxiety about re-entry to this school had been anticipated and discussed ahead of the meeting with Gina and her foster mother. Gina's characteristic pattern of response when anxious might also have been anticipated so that her foster mother was in less danger of being caught unawares. A fourth person, perhaps Gina's social worker or someone else she regarded as an ally could have joined the meeting so that she could feel well supported by someone she could experience as an ally.

Weak coalition between foster parents and birth parents. This is most likely to lead to a conflict of loyalty for the adolescent, unless they are totally unpreoccupied with their birth family at that point in time, which is relatively unusual. In Chapter 6 Lee Robinson contrasted the conflict of loyalty he experienced between his grandmother and foster parents who did not like each other with his brother's more comfortable experience of having his foster parents and birth family 'muddle together'. Had the two families been able to work together, they might have contained Lee's anxiety when he was banned by his school from meeting with his girlfriend who was under the age of sexual consent. This action triggered Lee's attachment behaviour, which took the form of him going missing with his girlfriend and making for his grandmother's house where they were kept in hiding. Lee was genuinely fond of his foster parents and found the conflict between the two families intolerable, and it was he who brought the placement to an end.

The social worker's task. Social workers may need to act as facilitators of collaboration or concilliators between foster parents and members of the adolescent's birth family. They will need to watch for developing conflict between the adults concerned, including conflict in which they find themselves lined up on one side of the argument. In order to remain effective, the social worker's role is to step in to hold the tensions within the caregiving team when the adolescent might otherwise split people apart. Many foster parents and birth parents find it very hard to maintain a neutral stance towards each other, and opportunities to air feelings of fury or dislike openly with a social worker without fear of criticism or over identification with their position can do much to enable them to continue to work together constructively.

Weak coalition between foster parents and social worker with stronger alliance or coalition between social worker and adolescent. When this happens the stronger alliance between the adolescent and one adult tends to set up rivalry between the adults concerned. This allows the adolescent to split ambivalent feelings when anxiety or anger reaches a certain threshold. At the end of Julie Piggott's placement, described in Chapter 7, the tension of three-way working could not be held, due largely to a conflict of views, values and strategy. Julie's foster mother favoured a gradual move out of the foster home, whereas her new social worker emphasised Julie's right to independence and to living her life as she pleased. The previous alliance between Julie and her foster mother had been reasonably strong, such that it had contained some conflict between them and they had managed to agree to differ. However, when the social worker took on the role of being a 'better parent' than Julie's foster mother a deep split developed between Julie and her foster mother which they seemed unable to repair once Julie had been moved out of her foster home into a bedsitter earlier than had been planned. Afterwards both Julie and her foster mother expressed regret at the precipitate move and a strong wish to get together, but seemed unable to do so.

The social worker's task. Here a secure base for the caregiving network would be constructed by a worker being present at, or, if necessary, convening meetings between foster mother, Julie's social worker and Julie. The task is to act as mediator and to hold onto the fact that there were probably points for and against both views. The aim would be for Julie to experience both foster parent and social worker as being concerned for her interests and intent on enabling her to weigh up the pro's and cons of moving out or staying put for longer.

If conflict can be contained and held within the part of the caregiving network where it is being experienced, there is a chance that the adolescent may be able to internally reformulate the elements of disastrous conflict within their internal working models and 'forgive' earlier attachment figures.

Summary

In order to offer foster families and the wider caregiving network the experience of a secure base from which they can work effectively with adolescents in their care, social workers must be regularly and readily available to members of the network. Their work is likely to be mainly with foster parents, as they are the direct caregivers, but will also aim to enable members and subsystems of the network to work together in the adolescent's best interests. When they are able to do this members of the caregiving network will be providing a secure base for each other.

This work needs to be undertaken by a social worker who is not responsible for the adolescent; the task is far too demanding to be taken on by the adolescent's social worker, and it is a near impossible task for the same worker to manage his or her own proximity behaviour appropriately, in relation to both the adolescent and the network.

The skills and qualities required for constructing a secure base for the caregiving network can be summarised under four headings:

Empathy. This involves the social worker offering foster parents and other caregivers their full attention, in their own right, so that they can be encouraged to explore and communicate their real feelings about what is happeneing in the placement, including their worst fears. This requires very careful listening and a nonjudgemental attitude on the part of the social worker. The aim is to enable the caregiver to regain their reflective stance towards the adolescent, in which conflicts and dilemmas can be acknowledged. Together, it will then be possible to express and explore negative feelings triggered by the adolescent and to bear the risks and uncertainties of this very demanding form of care. Empathy will go far to assuage an anxious or angry caregiver's attachment behaviour which will be preventing them from working effectively with the adolescent.

Encouraging open communication. It will help to keep communication between all concerned open and explicit, this is particularly important when communication becomes blocked for fear of conflict, or when a caregiver is operating on a hidden agenda of which they may not be fully aware. If the social worker is experienced as a secure base then risky communication can be tried out with him or her first before any attempt is made to bring the non-communicating parties together. There are times when the social worker may act as mediator.

Practical support in alliance formation. When building a good working alliance between adolescent and foster parent is regarded as a task of first importance, foster parents may find themselves called upon to take responsibility in situations that are unfamiliar to them; meeting careers officers or employers, or helping to find lodgings, for example. When it is in the service of the alliance for adolescent and foster parents to do important things together, the social worker's role may be to provide the practical know-how to foster parents, rather than doing the job themselves. They may also need to provide additional services to foster parents to free them to take on these new roles. As well as practice implications there are important policy and financial implications if foster parents are to have the time, space and emotional energy to continue to work with adolescents who have left the placement.

Reaffirming foster parents' value to the adolescent. Standing at one remove from the direct caregiving, it is more possible for social workers to monitor changes and positive progress and to be clear what it is that foster parents are doing that is helping. It is very important that this is communicated to the foster parents, who are often too close to what is happening to be sure of the value of what they are doing, particularly when they are working with an angry or emotionally detached adolescent who has difficulty in affirming their caregivers. Positive reframing of behaviour can be helpful, but where a foster parent's view that an adolescent is totally unable to make positive use of the placement is well supported, this should, of course be taken seriously.

Supervision or consultation: a secure base for the social worker

Social workers, in common with foster parents and the adolescents they foster, must also have a secure base from which to undertake this very demanding and highly skilled job. It is essential that they have access to skilled professional supervision or consultation on a regular basis. It will be found that the processes within supervision and consultation that enable practitioners to bear the emotional pain of those who are insecurely attached, and to work creatively with them and their caregivers, follow similar principles to those outlined in this book.

Epilogue

Adolescents who are separated from their birth families are likely to continue to be a source of concern and anxiety to social work agencies. Many return home without any of their difficulties resolved or alternatively struggle to survive on their own, unable or unwilling to turn to anyone who might help when they encounter problems. Despite their hopes and efforts as adult partners and parents to create a better life for their children than they themselves experienced, many find themselves caught up in similar patterns of distorted attachment.

The majority of adolescents in care do not wish to be placed with a new family on a permanent basis; previous experience of family life results in many being apprehensive about family placement, even on a time limited basis and the breakdown rates for adolescents in such placements are higher than for younger children (Berridge and Cleaver, 1987). Nevertheless, as Stein and Carey's (1986) research demonstrated so clearly, the majority do want at least one person who will be reliably available for them, who will be welcoming, tolerant and understanding, and who will listen carefully to them and respond to them with empathy and sensitivity. There is widespread evidence from practice that adolescent fostering projects are an effective way of offering adolescents that opportunity and through it, the secure base they need if they are to successfully negotiate the transition to adult life. Those adolescents whose previous experience leaves them

unable to contemplate living in a foster family, al
quality of care identified in this study if they are to a
life with confidence and with the ability to turn to peo
can trust when they need support.

By studying the interaction between adolescents and
parents during placements and making sense of wha
from the perspective of attachment theory, it has been po
show that adolescents are able to make changes in the way they
perceive and relate to significant others within the context of
foster family life, and that these changes are not due to chance but
to the way foster parents relate to them and work with them. Once
the relationship difficulties that frequently develop between
adolescents and their foster parents and which threaten the
continuing viability of placements are understood, they may also
be regarded as the focus for change and growth. When an
adolescent is able to experience members of their foster family as
a secure base and provided the foster family continues to be
available and accessible to the adolescent when the placement
ends, there appears to be a reasonable likelihood of these
adolescents and young adults being able to develop different
patterns of attachment and parental behaviour than those they
have experienced themselves as children.

Demand always outstrips supply and far more foster parents are
needed for adolescents. Moreover if residential care was to be
staffed, organised and financed in such a way that it became
possible for staff to provide a similar quality of care, based on
these principles, then that would offer adolescents a viable
alternative to foster care and a real choice. At present this choice is
all too often not available.

In this context it is essential to realise that if placement in foster
care is an emotionally demanding route into adult life for the
adolescents concerned, it is at least equally so for foster parents
and social workers. This form of care, whether provided by foster
parents or by caregivers in a residential setting, cannot be provided
inexpensively and it is labour intensive. It requires specialist
training for foster parents, other caregivers and social workers and
an organisational structure which supports developing expertise.
Payment of foster parents and other caregivers needs to recognize
the highly skilled work they do, if sufficient numbers are to be
recruited, sustained and offered space and recovery time between

...ments. There also needs to be sufficient specialist social work staff who are able to work flexibly and creatively with foster parents as colleagues and to construct a secure base for foster parents and other caregivers concerned with each placement if they are to work together effectively in the interests of the adolescent.

Bibliography

Ainsworth, M.D.S., Blehar, M.C., Waters, E. and Wall, S. (1978), *Patterns of Attachment: A Psychological Study of the Strange Situation,* Erlbaum, Hillsdale, N.J.

Aldgate, J., Maluccio, A., and Reeves C. (1989), *Adolescents and Foster Families,* B.T.Batsford Ltd in association with British Agencies for Adoption and Fostering, London.

Berridge, D. (1985) *Children's Homes,* Basil Blackwell, Oxford.

Berridge, D. and Cleaver H. (1987), *Foster Home Breakdown,* Basil Blackwell, Oxford.

Bingley, L., Loader, P.J. and Kinston W. (1984), 'Research Report: Further development of a format for family description', *Australian Journal of Family Therapy,* vol.5, no.3, pp.215-218.

Bowlby, J. (1973), *Attachment and Loss,* vol.2: *Separation: Anxiety and Anger,* The Hogarth Press and The Institute of Psycho-Analysis, London.

Bowlby, J. (1988), 'On knowing what you are not supposed to know and feeling what you are not supposed to feel', in *A Secure Base: Clinical Applications of Attachment Theory,* Routledge, London.

Bretherton, I. (1990a), 'Communication patterns, internal working models and the intergenerational transmission of attachment relationships', *Infant Mental Health Journal,* vol.11, no.3, Fall, pp 237-252.

Bretherton, I. (1990b), 'Open communication and internal working models: their role in the development of attachment relationships' in Thompson, R. (ed), *Socioemotional Development (Nebraska Symposium on Motivation 1988),* University of Nebraska Press, Lincoln, Nebraska.

Burgess, C. (1981), *In Care and Into Work,* Tavistock Publications, London.

Byng-Hall, J. (1988), 'Scripts and Legends in Families and Family Therapy', *Family Process,* vol.27, pp.167-179.

197

Byng-Hall, J. (1990), 'Attachment Theory and Family Therapy: A Clinical View', *Infant Mental Health Journal,* vol.11, no.3, Fall, pp.228-236.

Byng-Hall, J. and Campbell D., (1981), 'Resolving conflicts in family distance regulation: an integrative approach', *Journal of Marital and Family Therapy,* Summer.

Caplan, G. (1964), *Principles of Preventive Psychiatry,* Tavistock Publications, London.

Carey, K. and Stein, M. (1984), *A Study of Young People Leaving Care,* End of Grant Report, University of Leeds.

Cautley, P.(1980), *New Foster Parents: The First Experience,* Human Sciences Press, New York.

Cooper, J. (1978), *Patterns of Family Placement,* National Children's Bureau, London.

Corrigan, M. and Floud, C. (1990), 'A framework for direct work with children in care', *Adoption and Fostering,* vol.14, no.3, pp.28-32.

Crittenden, P.(1985), 'Maltreated Infants: Vunerability and Resilience', *Journal of Child Psychology and Psychiatry,* vol.26, no.1, pp.85-96.

Department of Health, (1991), *The Children Act: Guidance and Regulations,* Vol.3, *Family Placements,* HMSO, London.

DHSS, (1984), *A Study of Specialist Fostering in Essex,* Social Work Service, DHHS, London.

Downes, C. (1986), The Reparative Potential of Foster family Interaction: Difficult Adolescents in *Time Limited Placements,* Unpublished D.Phil. Thesis, University of York.

Downes, C. (1987), 'Fostered teenagers and children in the family', *Adoption and Fostering,* vol.11, no.4, pp.11-16.

Downes, C. (1988), 'Foster Families for Adolescents: the healing potential of time limited placements', *British Journal of Social Work,* vol.18, no.5, October, pp.473-487.

Fahlberg, V. (1981a) *Attachment and separation,* British Agencies for Adoption and Fostering, practice series 5, London.

Fahlberg, V. (1981b) *Helping children when they must move,* British Agencies for Adoption and Fostering, practice series 6, London.

Fahlberg, V. (1982), *Child development,* British Agencies for Adoption and Fostering, practice series 7, London.

Fahlberg, V. (1988), *The child in placement: common behavioural problems,* British Agencies for Adoption and Fostering, practice series 16, London.

Fanshel, D. and Shinn, E.B. (1978), *Children in Foster Care: a longitudinal investigation,* Columbia University Press, New York.

George, C., Kaplan, N. and Main, M. (1985), 'An Adult Attachment Interview: Interview Protocol', Unpublished manuscript, Department of Psychology, University of California, Berkeley.

Godek, S. (1976), *Leaving Care,* Barnardo Social Work Paper, no.2, Barkingside, Essex.

Greenberg, M.T., Siegel, J.M. and Leitch, C.J. (1983) 'The Nature and Importance of Attachment Relationships to Parents and Peers During Adolescence', *Journal of Youth and Community*, vol.12, no.5, pp 373-386.

Hansburg, H.G. (1980a), *Adolescent Separation Anxiety*, vol.1: *A Method for the Study of Adolescent Separation Problems*, Robert E. Krieger Publishing Co., New York.

Hansburg, H.G. (1980b), *Adolescent Separation Anxiety*, vol.2: *Adolescent Separation Disorders*, Robert E. Krieger Publishing Co., New York.

Hapgood, M. (1988), 'Creative Direct Work with Adolescents: The Story of Craig Brooks' in Aldgate, J. and Simmonds, J. (eds), *Direct Work with Children: A Guide for Social Work Practitioners*, B.T. Batsford Ltd. in association with British Agencies for Adoption and Fostering, London.

Hazel, N. (1981) *A Bridge to Independence*, Blackwell, Oxford.

Heard, D.H. (1974), 'Crisis Intervention Guided by Attachment Concepts - a case study', *Journal of Child Psychology and Psychiatry*, vol.15, pp.111-122.

Heard,D.H. (1978), 'From Object Relations to Attachment Theory: A basis for family therapy', *British Journal of Medical Psychology*, vol.51, pp.67-76.

Heard, D.H. (1982), 'Family systems and the attachment dynamic', *Journal of Family Therapy*, vol.4, pp.99-116.

Heard, D.H. and Lake, B. (1986), 'The Attachment Dynamic in Adult Life', *British Journal of Psychiatry*, vol.149, pp.430-438.

Hipgrave, T. (1989), 'Concepts of parenting and adolescence – implications for fostering adolescents' in Aldgate, J., Maluccio, A. and Reeves, C. (eds), *Adolescents in Foster Families*, B.T.Batsford Ltd. in association with British Agencies for Adoption and Fostering, London.

Hodges, J. and Tizard, B. (1989), 'Social and Family Relationships of Ex-Institutional Adolescents', *Journal of Child Psychology and Psychiatry*, vol.30, no.1, pp.77-97.

Hoghughi, M. and Hipgrave, T. (1985), *Towards a discipline of fostering*, National Foster Care Association, London.

Holman, R. (1975), 'The place of fostering in social work', *British Journal of Social Work*, vol.5, no.1 pp.3-30.

Holman, R. (1980), 'Exclusive and inclusive concepts of fostering' in Triseliotis, J. (ed), *New developments in Foster care and Adoption*, Routledge and Kegan Paul, London.

Jewitt, C. (1984), *Helping Children Cope with Separation and Loss*, B.T.Batsford Ltd. in association with British Agencies for Adoption and Fostering, London.

Kälveston, A.L. (1976), *Caring for children with special needs*, Institut Européen Interuniversitaire de l'Action Sociale, Marcinelle, Belgium.

Kobak, R.R. and Sceery, A. (1988), 'Attachment in Late Adolescence, Working Models, Affect Regulation and Representation of Self and Others', *Child Development*, vol.59, pp.135-146.

Lupton, C. (1985), *Moving Out, Older Teenagers Leaving Residential Care,* Social Services Research and Intelligence Unit, Report no.12, Portsmouth.

Macaskill, C. (1986), 'Post Adoption Support' in Wedge, P.and Thoburn, J. (eds), *Finding families for 'hard-to-place' children: evidence from research,* British Agencies for Adoption and Fostering, research series 4, London.

Main, M. (1991), 'Metacognitive knowledge, metacognitive monitoring, and singular (coherent) vs. multiple (incoherent) model of attachment. Findings and directions for future research', in Parkes, C.M., Stevenson-Hinde, J. and Marris, P.(eds), *Attachment Across the Life Cycle,* Routledge, London.

Main, M. and Goldwyn, R. (1984), 'Predicting rejection of her infants from mother's representation of her own experiences: implications for the abused-abusing intergenerational cycle', *International Journal of Child Abuse and Neglect,* vol.8, pp.203-217.

Main, M. and Goldwyn, R. (1989), 'Adult Attachment Rating and Classification System', Unpublished scoring manual, Department of Psychology, University of California, Berkeley.

Main, M. and Hesse, E. (1990), 'Parents unresolved traumatic experiences are related to infant disorganised attachment status: is frightened and/or frightening parental behaviour the linking mechanism?' in Greenberg, M., Cicchetti, D. and Cummings, M. (eds), *Attachment in the Pre-School Years,* University of Chicago Press, Chicago.

Main, M., Kaplan, N. and Cassidy J. (1985), 'Security in Infancy, Childhood and Adulthood: A Move to the Level of Representation' in Bretherton, I. and Waters, E. (eds), *Growing Points in Attachment Theory and Research,* Monographs of the Society for Research in Child Development, Serial No.209, vol.50, nos. 1-2, The University of Chicago Press, Chicago.

Maizels, J. (1970), *Adolescent Needs and the Transition from School to Work,* Athlone Press, London.

Merton, R. (1957), *Social Theory and Social Structure,* Free Press, Glencoe, Illinois.

Milham, S., Bullock, R. and Hosie, K. (1978), *Locking up Children: secure provision within the child care system,* Saxon House, Farnborough.

Minuchin, P.(1985), 'Families and individual development: provocations from the field of family therapy', *Child Development,* vol.55, pp.289-302.

Minuchin, S. (1974), *Families and Family Therapy,* Harvard University Press, Cambridge, Massachusetts.

Parker, R.A. (1966), *Decision in Child Care,* Allen and Unwin, London.

Parkes, C.M. (1971), 'Psychosocial transitions: a field for study', *Social Science and Medicine,* vol.5, pp.101-115.

Paull, J.E. (1956), 'The Runaway Foster Child', *Child Welfare,* vol.35, no.7, July, pp.21-26.

Reid, W.J. and Epstein, L. (1972), *Task Centred Casework,* Columbia University Press, New York.

Rickford, F. (1991), 'No place like home', *Social Work Today,* vol.23, no.16, December 12th.

Ricks, M.H. (1985), 'The Social Transmission of Parental Behaviour: Attachment Across Generations' in Bretherton, I. and Waters, E. (eds), *Growing Points of Attachment Theory and Research,* Monographs of the Society for Research in Child Development, Serial No.209, vol.50, nos. 1-2, The University of Chicago Press, Chicago.

Rowe, J., Hundleby, M. and Garnett, L. (1989), *Child care now: a survey of placement patterns,* British Agencies for Adoption and Fostering, research series 6, London.

Rushton, A., Treseder, J., and Quinton, D. (1988), *New Parents for Older Children,* British Agencies for Adoption and Fostering, discussion series 10, London.

Ryan, T. and Walker, R. (1985), *Making Life Story Books,* British Agencies for Adoption and Fostering, London.

Sayer, T., Crouch, M., Geyer-Akers. and Gould, D. (1982), *The 16+ Project,* Barnardo Social Work Paper, no.15, Barkingside, Essex.

Shaw, M. and Hipgrave, T. (1982), 'Specialist Fostering: A Review of the Current Scene', *Adoption and Fostering,* vol.6, no.4, pp.21-25.

Shaw, M. and Hipgrave, T. (1983), *Specialist Fostering,* Batsford Academic and Educational Ltd. in association with British Agencies for Adoption and Fostering, London.

Sinason, V. (1990), 'Passionate Lethal Attachments', *British Journal of Psychotherapy,* vol.7, no.1.

Sinclair, I.A.C. (1971) *Hostels for Probationers,* HMSO, London.

Skynner, A.C.R. (1974), 'Boundaries', *Social Work Today,* vol.5, no.10, August 22nd, pp.290-294.

Smith, P.M. (1986), 'Evaluation of Kent Placements', *Adoption and Fostering,* vol.10, no.1, pp.29-33.

Stein, M. and Carey, K. (1986), *Leaving Care,* Basil Blackwell, Oxford.

Thoburn, J. (1988), *Child Placement: Principles and Practice,* Community Care Practice Handbook, Wildwood House, Aldershot.

Trasler, G. (1960), *In Place of Parents,* Routledge and Kegan Paul, London.

Winnicott, D.W. (1958), 'Hate in the Countertransference' in Winnicott, D.W., *Collected Papers: Through Paediatrics to Psycho-Analysis,* Tavistock Publications, London.

Winnicott, D.W. (1974), *Playing and Reality,* Penguin Books Ltd, Harmondsworth.

Woodhouse, D. and Pengelly, P.(1991), *Anxiety and the Dynamics of Collaboration,* Aberdeen University Press, Aberdeen.

Yelloly, M. (1979), *Independent Evaluation of Twenty Five Placements,* Kent Social Services Department, Maidstone.

Index of adolescents

Prospective sample

Retrospective sample

NOTTINGHAM UNIVERSITY LIBRARY